FINANCIAL INSTITUTIONS AND SERVICES

FINANCIAL STABILITY OVERSIGHT COUNCIL AND OFFICE OF FINANCIAL RESEARCH

ELEMENTS AND ASSESSMENTS

FINANCIAL INSTITUTIONS AND SERVICES

Additional books in this series can be found on Nova's website under the Series tab.

Additional E-books in this series can be found on Nova's website under the E-book tab.

BUSINESS ISSUES, COMPETITION AND ENTREPRENEURSHIP

Additional books in this series can be found on Nova's website under the Series tab.

Additional E-books in this series can be found on Nova's website under the E-book tab.

FINANCIAL INSTITUTIONS AND SERVICES

FINANCIAL STABILITY OVERSIGHT COUNCIL AND OFFICE OF FINANCIAL RESEARCH

ELEMENTS AND ASSESSMENTS

NOLAN S. COMPTON
EDITOR

nova publishers
New York

For permission to use material from this book please contact us:
Telephone 631-231-7269; Fax 631-231-8175
Web Site: http://www.novapublishers.com

Library of Congress Cataloging-in-Publication Data

ISBN: 978-1-62417-217-5

Published by Nova Science Publishers, Inc. † New York

CONTENTS

PREFACE

The 2007-2009 financial crisis focused attention on weaknesses in the U.S. regulatory structure, including the lack of an agency or mechanism responsible for monitoring and addressing risks across the financial system and a shortage of timely information to facilitate that oversight. In response to the crisis, Congress passed the Dodd-Frank Wall Street Reform and Consumer Protection Act (Dodd-Frank Act) in July 2010, which provided a broad range of regulatory reforms. Among many other things, the act established the Financial Stability Oversight Council (FSOC) to monitor the stability of the U.S. financial system and take actions to mitigate risks that might destabilize the system. This book provides an overview of elements and assessments of the Financial Stability Oversight Council and Office of Financial Research with a focus on Frequently Asked Questions.

Chapter 1 - In 2010, the Dodd-Frank Wall Street Reform and Consumer Protection Act created FSOC to identify and address threats to the stability of the U.S. financial system and OFR to support FSOC and Congress by providing financial research and data. GAO was asked to examine (1) any challenges FSOC and OFR face in fulfilling their missions (2) FSOC and OFR's efforts to establish management structures and mechanisms to carry out their missions, (3) FSOC and OFR's activities for supporting collaboration among their members and external stakeholders, and (4) the processes FSOC used to issue rules and reports.

GAO reviewed FSOC documents related to the annual reports, rulemakings, and committee procedures, as well as documents on OFR's budget, staffing, and strategic planning. GAO also interviewed FSOC and OFR staff, FSOC member and member agency staff, and external stakeholders, including foreign officials, industry trade groups, and academics.

Chapter 2 - The Financial Stability Oversight Council (FSOC) has a clear statutory mandate that creates for the first time collective accountability for identifying risks and responding to emerging threats to financial stability. It is a collaborative body chaired by the Secretary of the Treasury that brings together the expertise of the federal financial regulators, an insurance expert appointed by the President, and state regulators.

The FSOC has important new authorities to constrain excessive risk in the financial system. For instance, the FSOC has authority to designate a nonbank financial firm for tough new supervision and therefore avoid the regulatory gaps that existed before the recent crisis. Closing these gaps in supervision will help minimize the risk of a nonbank financial firm threatening the stability of the financial system.

Additionally, to help with the identification of emerging risks to financial stability, the FSOC can provide direction to, and request data and analyses from the newly created Office of Financial Research (OFR) housed within Treasury.

Chapter 3 - In establishing the Office of Financial Research (OFR or Office), the framers of the Dodd-Frank Wall Street Reform and Consumer Protection Act, Public Law 111-203 (Dodd-Frank Act) recognized the need for better data and better analysis to help the Financial Stability Oversight Council (Council) and market participants assess and respond to threats to financial stability.

Of course, there will always be a fundamental uncertainty about the source of such threats. But better data and analysis can support the design of stronger financial shock absorbers and guardrails to reduce the risk of crises. They can also support earlier warning and effective responses to mitigate the effects of crises when they do occur and help draw lessons for the future.

This strategic framework takes as its foundation the statutory mandates from the Dodd-Frank Act. It outlines a mission, goals, objectives and implementation priorities that will help to ensure that the OFR's efforts and investments are well targeted. It reflects substantial consultations in the period since enactment of the Dodd-Frank Act with a full range of stakeholders, including Council members, their agencies and staff, members of Congress, industry representatives, as well as academics, financial authorities, and other researchers.

An effective strategic framework involves adapting to changing circumstances, and the OFR must be nimble to achieve its mandate. The financial environment will continue to change rapidly, partly in response to an evolving regulatory architecture in the United States and around the globe. The

OFR will confront uncertainties inherent to new organizations undergoing rapid growth and change. Thus, this first articulation of the OFR strategic framework covers a shorter horizon than would be expected for a mature organization and frequent reviews and validation will be appropriate. The OFR will adapt this framework as necessary and undertake a first review in no later than two years.

Chapter 4 - The Dodd-Frank Wall Street Reform and Consumer Protection Act (Dodd-Frank), enacted July 21, 2010, created the Office of Financial Research (OFR) within the Department of the Treasury to support the Financial Stability Oversight Council (FSOC) and its member agencies. This chapter presents the results of the authors' audit of Treasury's activities to establish OFR as of April 2012.

In: Financial Stability Oversight Council ... ISBN: 978-1-62417-217-5
Editor: Nolan S. Compton

Chapter 1

FINANCIAL STABILITY: NEW COUNCIL AND RESEARCH OFFICE SHOULD STRENGTHEN THE ACCOUNTABILITY AND TRANSPARENCY OF THEIR DECISIONS*

United States Government Accountability Office

WHY GAO DID THIS STUDY

In 2010, the Dodd-Frank Wall Street Reform and Consumer Protection Act created FSOC to identify and address threats to the stability of the U.S. financial system and OFR to support FSOC and Congress by providing financial research and data. GAO was asked to examine (1) any challenges FSOC and OFR face in fulfilling their missions (2) FSOC and OFR's efforts to establish management structures and mechanisms to carry out their missions, (3) FSOC and OFR's activities for supporting collaboration among their members and external stakeholders, and (4) the processes FSOC used to issue rules and reports.

GAO reviewed FSOC documents related to the annual reports, rulemakings, and committee procedures, as well as documents on OFR's budget, staffing, and strategic planning. GAO also interviewed FSOC and

* This is an edited, reformatted and augmented version of the United States Government Accountability Office publication GAO-12-886, dated September 2012.

OFR staff, FSOC member and member agency staff, and external stakeholders, including foreign officials, industry trade groups, and academics.

WHAT GAO RECOMMENDS

GAO makes 10 recommendations to strengthen the accountability and transparency of FSOC and OFR's decisions and activities as well as to enhance collaboration among FSOC members and with external stakeholders. Treasury said, as Chairperson, that the council and OFR would consider the recommendations, but questioned the need for FSOC and OFR to clarify responsibilities for monitoring threats to financial stability and stated that OFR expects to share some risk indicators. However, stronger and more systematic actions are still needed in these areas.

WHAT GAO FOUND

These new organizations—the Financial Stability Oversight Council (FSOC) and Office of Financial Research (OFR)—face challenges in achieving their missions. Key FSOC missions—to identify risks and respond to emerging threats to financial stability—are inherently challenging, in part, because risks to financial stability do not develop in precisely the same way in successive crises. Collaboration among FSOC members can also be challenging at times, as almost all of them represent independent agencies that retained existing authorities. OFR faces the challenge of trying to establish and build a world-class research organization while meeting shorter-term goals and responsibilities.

FSOC's and OFR's management mechanisms to carry out their missions could be enhanced to provide greater accountability and transparency. FSOC and OFR have taken steps toward establishing such mechanisms. FSOC has established seven standing committees generally composed of staff of its members and member agencies to support the council in carrying out its business and provide information to the council for decision making and adopted a memorandum of understanding on information sharing to help govern its activities. FSOC and OFR have also issued annual reports on their activities and created web pages that provide some information to the public. However, certain mechanisms could be strengthened. For instance:

- FSOC's Systemic Risk Committee, which is responsible for identifying risks to financial stability, has procedures to facilitate analysis of risks raised by staff. However, without a more systematic approach and comprehensive information, FSOC member agencies, on their own, may not be well positioned to judge which potential threats will benefit from interagency discussions. GAO recommends that FSOC collect and share key financial risk indicators as part of a systematic approach to help identify potential threats to financial stability.
- Public information on FSOC's and OFR's decision making and activities is limited, which makes assessing their progress in carrying out their missions difficult. GAO recommends that (1) FSOC keep detailed records of closed-door sessions and (2) both entities develop a communication strategy to improve communications with the public.
- FSOC's annual reports—which serve as its key accountability documents—do not consistently identify which entities should monitor or implement the identified recommendations or give time frames for specific actions. To hold FSOC accountable for its recommendations, GAO recommends that FSOC recommend a lead agency or agencies to monitor or implement each recommendation within specified time frames.
- OFR issued a strategic framework in March 2012 as an important first step in adopting a strategic planning and performance management system. However, that document lacked some leading practices such as linking activities to strategic goals and performance measurement systems. GAO recommends that OFR further develop a strategic planning and performance management system that includes these elements and will allow it to be held accountable.

Although FSOC and OFR have taken steps to promote collaboration among FSOC members and external stakeholders, FSOC could further adopt key practices. FSOC member agency staff noted that agencies have leveraged their joint expertise and resources to produce FSOC's mandated reports and rules. OFR has also taken steps to collaborate with external stakeholders by initiating a working paper series, moving to form an advisory committee, and coordinating U.S. efforts at the international level to help create a legal entity identifier for financial entities that could enable regulators to identify parties to financial transactions. However, FSOC could do more to promote collaboration. For instance, FSOC, and OFR are required to monitor risks to financial stability, but they have not yet clarified agency responsibilities for implementation—creating the potential for regulatory gaps or duplication of effort. In addition, FSOC could take better advantage of statutory mechanisms to leverage external resources, including developing advisory committees. To improve collaboration and coordination among its member agencies and with external stakeholders, GAO recommends that FSOC (1) develop policies to clarify when formal collaboration or coordination should occur and FSOC's role in such efforts, (2) more fully incorporate key practices for successful collaboration that GAO has previously identified, and (3) clarify roles and responsibilities for implementing requirements to monitor risks to the financial system.

FSOC has issued rules that improve the transparency of its processes, and statutorily mandated reports but has not established processes to help ensure that these will have their intended results. While FSOC has issued rules on processes for designating nonbank financial entities for additional oversight and intends to review certain aspects of those rules, it has not developed plans for comprehensively evaluating whether designations are having their intended impact—reducing threats to financial stability. The impact of the designations on the economy and the financial entities will depend, in part, on a number of rules being issued by independent FSOC member agencies that will be applied to those being designated. Without a comprehensive assessment of the impact of these rules that will require the cooperation of individual FSOC members, understanding whether the designations are having their intended impact will be difficult. GAO recommends that FSOC develop a comprehensive framework for assessing the impact of its designation decisions. In addition, FSOC has not developed a systematic forward-looking process for identifying potential emerging threats in its mandated annual reporting process. In particular, FSOC does not have processes for consistently identifying such threats, separating them from more current threats, or prioritizing them. Identifying a large number of threats—the 2011 report identified over 30—without prioritizing them makes focusing on those that are most important difficult for decisionmakers. The 2012 report also included many threats, and neither report separates current threats from those that are potentially emerging. To improve FSOC's annual reporting on potential emerging threats, GAO recommends that FSOC develop more systematic approaches that are forward looking and help to prioritize the threats.

ABBREVIATIONS

CFTC	Commodity Futures Trading Commission
CIGFO	Council of Inspectors General on Financial Oversight
Dodd-Frank Act	Dodd-Frank Wall Street Reform and Consumer Protection Act
EU	European Union
Executive Orders	Executive Orders 12866 and 13563
FACA	Federal Advisory Committee Act
FDIC	Federal Deposit Insurance Corporation
Federal Reserve	Board of Governors of the Federal Reserve System
FFIEC	Federal Financial Institutions Examination Council
FMU	financial market utility
FOIA	Freedom of Information Act
FSOC	Financial Stability Oversight Council
GPRA	Government Performance and Results Act of 1993, as amended
G20	Group of 20
MOU	memorandum of understanding
NPR	notice of proposed rulemaking
OCC	Office of the Comptroller of the Currency
OFR	Office of Financial Research
OIG	Treasury Office of the Inspector General
SEC	Securities and Exchange Commission
Treasury	Department of the Treasury
UK	United Kingdom

September 11, 2012

The Honorable Spencer Bachus, Chairman
Committee on Financial Services
House of Representatives

The Honorable Randy Neugebauer, Chairman
Subcommittee on Oversight and Investigations
Committee on Financial Services
House of Representatives

The 2007-2009 financial crisis focused attention on weaknesses in the U.S. regulatory structure, including the lack of an agency or mechanism responsible for monitoring and addressing risks across the financial system and a shortage of timely information to facilitate that oversight. In response to the crisis, Congress passed the Dodd-Frank Wall Street Reform and Consumer Protection Act (Dodd-Frank Act) in July 2010, which provided for a broad range of regulatory reforms.[1] Among many other things, the act established the Financial Stability Oversight Council (FSOC) to monitor the stability of the U.S. financial system and take actions to mitigate risks that might destabilize the system.[2] The Dodd-Frank Act also created the Office of Financial Research (OFR) to support FSOC and Congress by providing financial research and data.[3] Congress gave FSOC a number of significant authorities to help it execute its broad mission, including to designate nonbank financial companies for heightened supervision by the Board of Governors of the Federal Reserve System (Federal Reserve) and to require financial companies to provide data to OFR. Congress set up some specific accountability mechanisms for FSOC and OFR, such as requiring annual reports and testimonies. However, some members have emphasized that to hold FSOC and OFR accountable, it needs to have a full understanding of the operations and decision making processes of these entities to help ensure that FSOC and OFR use their authorities as Congress intended.

To help provide oversight of FSOC and OFR, the Dodd-Frank Act gave GAO authority to audit these new entities, including their structures, staffing, and decision making processes. Under this authority, you asked us to examine the standing-up of these new entities. This report examines (1) any challenges FSOC and OFR face in fulfilling their missions; (2) FSOC's and OFR's efforts in establishing management structures and mechanisms to carry out their missions and attain their goals; (3) FSOC's and OFR's activities for supporting collaboration among members and external stakeholders, including international bodies and regulators; and (4) FSOC's processes used to issue rules and reports.

To identify and examine any challenges faced by FSOC and OFR, we reviewed our prior reports on financial reform and the 2007-2009 financial crisis and statements by government officials and academic experts. To assess their progress in establishing management structures and mechanisms, we reviewed documents and interviewed officials on FSOC's and OFR's missions, budgeting, staffing, data security, and planning. We assessed the reliability of OFR's staffing data and determined that the data were sufficiently reliable for the purposes of this report. In addition, we reviewed literature on tools used or proposed by entities that write financial stability reports, and others, to identify potential threats to financial stability. We also coordinated with the inspectors general from the Department of the Treasury (Treasury) and the Council of Inspectors General on Financial Oversight (CIGFO) on their reviews of OFR and FSOC, respectively.[4]

To evaluate FSOC's and OFR's activities for collaboration among members and external stakeholders, we analyzed FSOC policies, procedures, and products to determine whether and how their practices compared with key elements of effective collaboration we have previously identified.[5] We also reviewed selected documents from international bodies for evidence of changes in their dealings with U.S. financial regulators since FSOC's creation. To examine FSOC's processes for issuing rules and reports, we identified products that had been issued as of July 20, 2012, and reviewed the processes used to develop them. We compared documentary and testimonial information from Treasury officials with rulemaking criteria established in our prior work and with standard economic practice. For all objectives, we interviewed FSOC and OFR staff and officials from FSOC's member agencies. We also interviewed external stakeholders, including foreign officials, industry trade groups, and academics on various topics related to our objectives. For more information on our scope and methodology, see appendix I.

We conducted this performance audit from November 2011 to September 2012 in accordance with generally accepted government auditing standards. Those standards require that we plan and perform the audit to obtain sufficient, appropriate evidence to provide a reasonable basis for our findings and conclusions based on our audit objectives. We believe that the evidence obtained provides a reasonable basis for our findings and conclusions based on our audit objectives.

BACKGROUND

For some time, we have been reporting that the U.S. financial regulatory system has relied on a fragmented and complex arrangement of federal and state regulators to oversee its institutions.[6] This system—put into place over the last 150 years—has not kept pace with major developments in financial markets and products in recent decades. In particular, the current system was not designed to oversee today's large and interconnected financial institutions, whose activities pose new risks to the institutions themselves as well as to the broader financial system. This risk to the broader financial system, called systemic risk, refers to the possibility that a single event could broadly affect the entire financial system, causing widespread losses rather than just losses at one or a few institutions. Given these observations and concerns, we offered a framework for crafting and evaluating regulatory reform proposals that would have the characteristics that should be reflected in any new regulatory system.[7] For example, we said that a regulatory system should minimize regulatory burden and promote accountability. We also designated reforming the financial regulatory system as a high-risk area in 2009.[8]

FSOC's three primary purposes under the Dodd-Frank Act are to

1. identify risks to the financial stability of the United States that could arise from the material financial distress or failure, or ongoing activities, of large, interconnected bank holding companies and nonbank financial companies, as well as risks that could arise outside the financial services marketplace;
2. promote market discipline by eliminating expectations on the part of shareholders, creditors, and counterparties of these large companies that the U.S. government will shield them from losses in the event of failure; and
3. respond to emerging threats to the stability of the U.S. financial system.

To achieve these purposes, the Dodd-Frank Act gave FSOC a number of important authorities that allow it to

- collect information across the financial system so that regulators will be better prepared to address emerging threats;
- designate for supervision by the Federal Reserve those nonbank financial companies that pose risks to the financial system as defined by the act;
- designate as systemically important certain financial market utilities (FMU) and payment, clearing, or settlement activities, requiring them to meet prescribed risk management standards, and subjecting them to enhanced regulatory oversight;[9]
- recommend stricter standards for the large, interconnected bank holding companies and nonbank financial companies designated for enhanced supervision;

- vote on determination by the Federal Reserve that action should be taken to break up institutions that pose a "grave threat" to U.S. financial stability; and
- facilitate information sharing and coordination among the member agencies to eliminate gaps in the regulatory structure.[10]

FSOC is chaired by the Secretary of the Treasury. As the chairperson of FSOC, the Secretary has certain powers and responsibilities related to FSOC's meetings, rulemakings, recommendations, and reports and testimony to Congress. The Secretary, in consultation with the other FSOC members, is also responsible for regular consultation with the financial regulatory entities and other appropriate organizations of foreign governments or international organizations. As shown in figure 1, the Dodd-Frank Act provides that FSOC consists of 10 voting members and 5 nonvoting members. The 10 voting members provide a federal regulatory perspective and an independent insurance expert's view. The 5 nonvoting members offer different insights as state-level representatives from bank, securities, and insurance regulators or as the directors of some new offices within Treasury—OFR and the Federal Insurance Office—that were established by the Dodd-Frank Act. The Dodd-Frank Act requires that the council meet at least once a quarter.

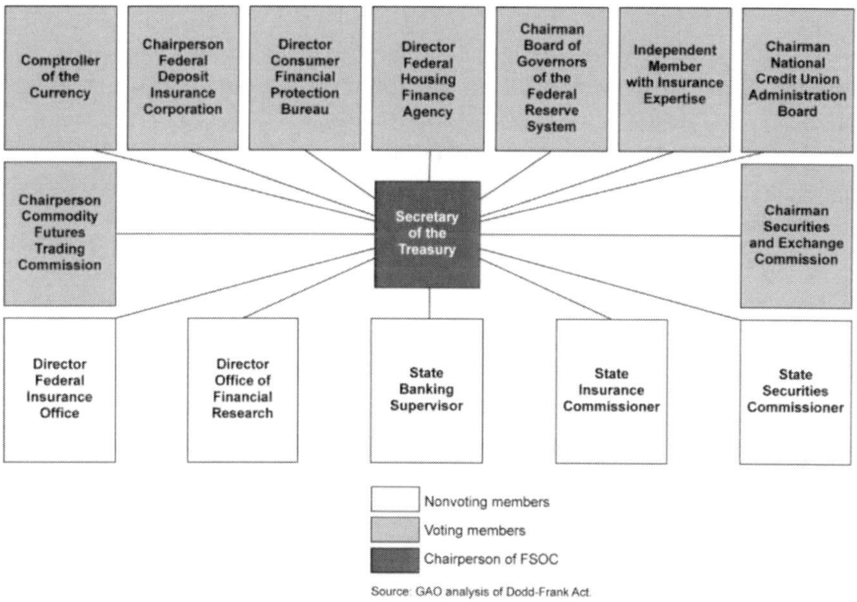

Figure 1. FSOC Membership.

The Dodd-Frank Act established OFR to serve FSOC and its member agencies by improving the quality, transparency, and accessibility of financial data and information, conducting and sponsoring research related to financial stability, and promoting best practices in risk management. The act requires OFR to set up a data center and a research and analysis center to, among other things,

- collect and provide data to FSOC and member agencies;
- standardize the types and formats of data reported and collected;
- perform applied and essential long-term research;
- develop tools for risk measurement and monitoring; and
- make the results of its activities available to financial regulatory agencies.

FSOC and OFR do not receive appropriated funds. During the 2-year period following the enactment of the Dodd-Frank Act, the Federal Reserve provided OFR funds to cover the expenses of the office. Moving forward, OFR will be funded through assessments levied on bank holding companies with total consolidated assets of $50 billion or more and nonbank financial companies designated by FSOC for supervision by the Federal Reserve.[11] Until FSOC finalizes its designations for nonbank financial companies, assessments will be levied only against large bank holding companies. The collected assessments will be deposited into the Financial Research Fund, which was established within Treasury to fund the expenses of OFR. FSOC's expenses are considered expenses of OFR. The President's fiscal year 2013 budget included estimates of about $123 million for the Financial Research Fund for fiscal year 2012 and about $158 million for fiscal year 2013. Most of these funds are to support OFR, but the estimates include about $8 million for FSOC operations in fiscal year 2012 and nearly $9 million in fiscal year 2013.[12] Most of OFR's funding is budgeted for contractual services—including reimbursable support from Treasury and administrative services from the Office of the Comptroller of the Currency (OCC) and the Bureau of Public Debt—employees and equipment.[13]

FSOC AND OFR FACE CHALLENGES ACHIEVING THEIR MISSIONS

Key FSOC missions—to identify risks to U.S. financial stability and respond to emerging threats to stability—are inherently challenging. Risks to the stability of the U.S. financial system are difficult to identify because key indicators, such as market prices, often do not reflect these risks. Further, such threats do not develop in precisely the same way in successive crises, making them harder to identify. As FSOC's chairperson acknowledged in FSOC's 2011 Annual Report, the most significant threats to the stability of the financial system will often be the ones that are hardest to diagnose and preempt. Moreover, financial innovations that are not well understood further complicate the challenge. For example, prior to the 2007-2009 financial crisis, some experts viewed the risks associated with falling housing prices as a regional phenomenon. With the advent of mortgage-backed securities, these experts believed that the danger that falling house prices posed on the regional level had been mitigated, as they thought these securities had diversified and dispersed the risks. Although this dispersion of risk was expected to limit the impact of regional downturns, it helped to transmit the downturn in housing prices across the financial system and the nation. Experts have also noted that the task of effectively monitoring and mitigating systemic risk is both vast and procedurally complex. Additionally, actions to preemptively mitigate threats may appear unnecessary or too costly at the time they are proposed or taken. Although achieving FSOC's key missions is inherently challenging, failure to achieve them will continue to leave the financial system vulnerable to large or multiple shocks that could result in the large losses in asset values, higher unemployment, and slower economic growth associated with previous financial crises.

Although the Dodd-Frank Act created FSOC to provide for a more comprehensive view of threats to U.S. financial stability, it left most of the fragmented and complex arrangement of independent Federal and State regulators that existed prior to the Dodd-Frank Act in place and generally preserved their statutory responsibilities. As a result, FSOC's effectiveness hinges to a large extent on collaboration among its many members, almost all of whom come from state and federal agencies with their own specific statutory missions. In testifying on the coordination of Dodd-Frank rulemakings assigned to specific FSOC members, before the U.S. House Financial Services Committee in October 2011, the chairperson of FSOC recognized this challenge. He noted that the coordination challenge in the rulemaking process was hard because the Dodd-Frank Act left in place a financial system with a complicated set of independent agencies with overlapping jurisdictions and different responsibilities. However, the Chairperson also noted that certain agencies were working much more closely together than they did before the creation of FSOC. In our prior work, the federal financial regulators also emphasized the importance of maintaining their independence while serving as members of FSOC. For example, several FSOC member agencies noted in our prior work on Dodd-Frank rulemakings that any effort to coordinate rulemakings assigned to specific agencies through FSOC would need to be balanced against the statutory requirements of the independent agencies involved.[14] In addition, the Chairperson has similarly noted that he does not have the authority to force agencies to coordinate, and neither he, nor FSOC as a whole, can force agencies to adopt compatible policies and procedures. FSOC members' staffs and staff at member agencies also noted that differences in policies and procedures are designed to address the differences in the entities they regulate. Regulators have also pointed to their differing statutory requirements to explain why they have differing views on policy issues. During the Basel II deliberations, for instance, U.S. bank regulators—the Federal Deposit Insurance Corporation (FDIC), Federal Reserve, and OCC—each had a different view of various aspects of those requirements.[15] The regulators traced their differences back to their specific statutory responsibilities. Furthermore, although the United Kingdom (UK) and the European Union (EU) have established or are in the process of establishing councils to oversee systemic risk, in the UK and the EU the central bank has more members or more votes than other entities on these councils. In contrast, in the United States, the central bank—the Federal Reserve—has one member on FSOC and one vote among the 10 voting members. FSOC policy staff and staff at member agencies noted that the diverse perspectives of FSOC members enrich FSOC deliberations.

OFR also faces the challenge of trying to build a world-class research organization from the ground up while meeting shorter term goals and responsibilities. Recognizing these difficulties, the Dodd-Frank Act required that OFR submit annual human resource planning reports to Congress that cover the new entity's plans for recruitment and retention, training and workforce development, and workforce flexibility. The September 2011 plan stated that a key feature of the recruitment message was to highlight OFR's ability to engage top academic and industry professionals through several unique opportunities. These included the ability to work in innovative research networks and with unique data sets, as well as the historic opportunity to be involved from the beginning in a new institution with broad, challenging goals. OFR recognizes the challenge of attracting and retaining highly trained staff, who often have other employment alternatives. When asked about challenges they face, OFR officials noted that one challenge to starting a research organization that is an unknown entity derives, in part, from some prospective employees wanting to see which other researchers are in place before agreeing to an employment offer. OFR officials told us that the organization is making steady progress toward reaching a point at which it will have an established core of staff and greater name recognition that will lessen this challenge. Those researchers who supported the creation of OFR have suggested that it will take many years for the new entity to provide the insights that will ultimately be expected of it. These researchers have also noted that the absence of a director for the organization has slowed this process. At the same time that OFR faces the long-term challenges of building a world-class research organization, it also faces the challenge of balancing this longer-term goal with the need to meet shorter-term goals such as providing ongoing support to FSOC and standardizing the types and format of data collected and reported by the financial regulatory agencies.[16]

FSOC's and OFR's Management Structures and Mechanisms Could be Enhanced to Provide Greater Accountability and Transparency

FSOC and OFR have taken steps toward meeting the challenges they face, including setting up their management structures, communicating their mission and goals, and hiring staff. However, both entities could enhance their accountability mechanisms and level of transparency. FSOC and OFR have also taken steps to build mechanisms to identify potential threats to financial stability, but additional actions would strengthen this key mission of both entities. Additionally, while FSOC and OFR have developed web pages on Treasury's website and taken other steps to provide information to the public, these efforts have limitations and do not always fully inform Congress or the public about their activities and progress. Without taking additional steps to improve accountability and transparency, FSOC and OFR are missing the opportunity to demonstrate their progress in carrying out their missions.

FSOC and OFR Have Set up Initial Structures and Hired Staff, but Some Key Leadership Positions Remain Vacant at OFR

As we have reported in the past, agencies can manage or mitigate many of the challenges of setting up new organizations by developing strong management structures and control mechanisms.[17] The literature on control mechanisms and government performance suggests that certain mechanisms, such as setting out goals and linking staffing, activities, and budgets to them, are key even when new agencies are being formed.[18] Such control mechanisms provide management, staff, stakeholders, and the public with a good understanding of the organization's mission and goals, the steps it intends to take to carry out those goals, and an ongoing level of accountability. Agencies also need to establish measures to gauge their performance so that they can change strategies that are deficient in a timely manner. Organizations must also maintain an appropriate level of transparency. Because certain agencies rely on confidential information, such as that obtained during regulatory supervision, an appropriate level of transparency recognizes the need to maintain confidentiality and information security. In addition, agencies must balance the need for transparency with the need for those involved in deliberations to be able to express their views.

FSOC has begun setting up its management structures. It has established a dedicated policy office within Treasury's Office of Domestic Finance, led by a Deputy Assistant Secretary, which functions as the FSOC Secretariat. Among other duties, the policy office works with staff of other FSOC members to support FSOC in its day-to-day operations by helping to draft rules, studies, and reports and prepare and circulate relevant materials to agency members prior to council meetings. The office also serves as a mechanism to bring issues to the council quickly. As of June 2012, there were 25 staff members in the FSOC policy office.

FSOC has established seven standing committees generally composed of staff of its members and member agencies to carry out the business of the council including developing the information the members need to make decisions effectively. The Deputies Committee, which meets every 2 weeks and consists of senior officials designated by members, is responsible for coordinating and overseeing the work of the staff committees. The deputies may resolve issues that arise in the other committees and determine the information that needs to be passed on to the FSOC members for discussion. Some other committees include the Systemic Risk Committee that analyzes emerging threats to financial stability, designations committees that support

FSOC in evaluating FMUs and nonbank financial companies for certain additional oversight, and the Data Committee that supports OFR's data collection efforts.[19] FSOC policy staff stated that all members and member agencies were invited to have staff participate on any committee and, in some cases, FSOC members attend committee meetings as well. They also noted that ad hoc staff groups were formed periodically to work on issues that might not fit within the purview of a standing committee. For example, an ad hoc group helped draft FSOC's 2011 Annual Report, and an ongoing legal working group holds conference calls as needed to address legal issues.

OFR has also taken steps to set up needed management structures. As shown in figure 2, OFR has developed an organizational structure that is built around a Data Center and Research and Analysis Center—the two programmatic units established by the Dodd-Frank Act. OFR has adopted certain hiring policies required under the Dodd-Frank Act, including special salary schedules that are higher than the General Schedule, and used Treasury's existing authority from the Office of Personnel Management for Schedule A excepted hiring.[20] In testimony delivered to the House Financial Services Subcommittee on Oversight and Investigations, in April 2012, the Chief Operating Officer described plans to build up to a staffing level of from 275 to 300 staff in the next 2 to 3 years. OFR officials noted that they had relied on a variety of tools to solicit applicants, including letters to academic institutions. OFR's recruitment message has highlighted the opportunity to work on unique data sets and the historic opportunity to build a new institution that would promote financial stability. As of August 15, 2012 OFR had 112 employees. About three-quarters of these employees were direct hires (including 22 reimbursable staff from other Treasury departments) with the other quarter a combination of external detailees and student interns. Although this level is below the target employment level in OFR's budget, it represents marked progress from the second quarter of 2011, when OFR had seven employees and relied mostly on nonpermanent staff.

As it is for any agency, having effective leadership is critical to hiring qualified staff and providing effective governance. OFR has filled five of its eight top leadership positions, but two of the most important positions are not permanently filled: the OFR director and the deputy director of the Research and Analysis Center. A former Treasury official with knowledge of the search process for the director position said that it was difficult to attract a qualified candidate to head the agency for a 6-year term. After 17 months, the President put forth a nominee to head OFR in December 2011 who had been serving as the Counselor to the Secretary since April 2011 and continues to serve in that position. As of July 2012, the nominee is awaiting full Senate confirmation.[21] Since OFR has also not filled the deputy director position at the Research and Analysis Center, the Chief of Analytical Strategy has assumed responsibility for standing up the Research and Analysis Center, including overseeing the hiring process, determining data needs, and defining the center's objectives and strategy. In June, OFR filled the Data Center Deputy Director position by promoting the Chief Business Officer to this position. The new Data Center Deputy Director will continue to serve as the Acting Chief Business Officer until this position is filled. In addition to these vacancies, a number of lower-level management vacancies remain, including positions at the Research and Analysis Center. For example, none of the assistant director positions under the Deputy Director of Research and Analysis have been filled. In addition, two of five assistant director positions under the Chief Technology Officer are open. However, OFR is not actively looking to fill one of the assistant director positions until the office reaches a mature state and has the need for this additional position.

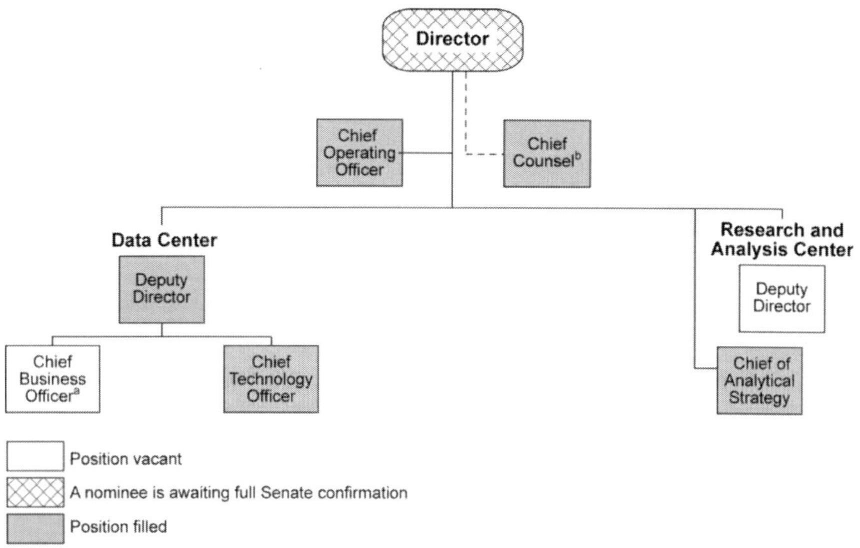

Source: GAO presentation of OFR information.

[a] The Deputy Director of the Data Center is also serving as the Acting Chief Business Officer.

[b] The Chief Counsel reports directly to Treasury's Office of General Counsel.

Figure 2. OFR Organizational Chart, as of July 2012.

FSOC and OFR Have Adopted Certain Policies but Could Strengthen Mechanisms to Fully Ensure Accountability and Transparency

FSOC has implemented policies such as bylaws, a transparency policy, and a consultation framework, and members have signed a memorandum of understanding (MOU) on sharing confidential information to govern FSOC activities and promote accountability and transparency. OFR has also adopted policies and procedures for its operations.

- FSOC's bylaws describe the duties of the Chairperson, members of the council, and staff; provide the governance structure for council meetings; and describe some policies for confidentiality and access to information, among other things. The bylaws also allow the Chairperson to appoint, with council approval, an Executive Director and Legal Counsel and to delegate some responsibilities to the Executive Director. As of July 2012, no one had been appointed to these positions. Instead, Treasury staff perform duties associated with these positions, such as providing ethics information to FSOC members.
- The transparency policy commits FSOC to holding at least two open meetings per year but also establishes reasons why other meetings might be closed. For example, meetings may be closed during discussions of supervisory or other market-sensitive information or if an open meeting would result in the disclosure of information contained in investigation, examination, operating, or condition reports; or would necessarily and significantly compromise the mission or purposes of FSOC if it were disclosed. The policy also states that FSOC will release minutes to the public after the meetings.
- FSOC's framework for consultation applies to regulations or actions required by the Dodd-Frank Act that must be completed in consultation with FSOC. For example, under the act, the Securities and Exchange Commission (SEC) must consult with FSOC in determining what information is to be collected from certain investment advisers to private funds relating to the assessment of systemic risk. The framework provides a timeline for holding initial meetings, circulating and commenting on staff recommendations, and briefing key policy staff of interested FSOC members on those recommendations.

- FSOC members also signed an MOU to help ensure confidentiality of nonpublic information. The MOU requires that FSOC members not share this information with anyone outside their member agencies or otherwise specified support staff. Treasury officials and FSOC staff said that the MOU is necessary because it enables council members to share nonpublic information within the council and provides assurance to covered staff that they will not incur penalties for sharing information consistent with the MOU's terms. They noted, for example, that sharing certain supervisory information without such an agreement could carry severe penalties. In June 2012, CIGFO released a report on FSOC's controls over nonpublic information.[22] CIGFO found that to date FSOC had shared limited nonpublic information, but this situation will change as OFR builds its capacity. CIGFO also found differences in the way FSOC member agencies marked and handled nonpublic information and noted that not addressing these differences could pose risks to the senders and receivers of such information. The FSOC Data Committee has undertaken a project to address these issues.
- OFR has adopted policies and procedures for its operations, including those for data security, human resources, budget execution, and procurement. Because data operations are an important feature of OFR's operations, OFR officials said that they had spent significant time on data security architecture, looking at issues of confidentiality, user access, and cyber threats such as hacking. OFR has adopted Treasury procedures for ensuring data security and is expanding its security controls as necessary for OFR-specific systems and data, as well as for information sharing across FSOC member agencies. To further ensure confidentiality, they have also adopted postemployment restrictions, as required by the Dodd-Frank Act, stating that OFR employees generally may not be employed by or provide advice or consulting services to financial companies for one year after if they have had access to certain confidential information.

In addition, FSOC has some planning under way and OFR has taken some actions and planned others that are consistent with legal requirements or leading practices for new organizations relative to strategic planning and performance management. In our prior work, we have identified three key steps for successful results-oriented organizations—(1) defining clear missions and desired outcomes; (2) measuring performance to gauge progress; and (3) using performance as a basis for decision making.[23] These practices are consistent with the Government Performance and Results Act of 1993, as amended (GPRA), which requires agencies to periodically produce strategic plans, annual performance plans, and performance updates.[24] FSOC, which is subject to GPRA, is in the early planning stages of how to satisfy its requirements and may, given its relatively small monetary outlays, request an exemption from certain GPRA requirements from the Office of Management and Budget.[25] In the interim, Treasury's strategic plan for fiscal year 2012-2015 describes FSOC and the Treasury Secretary's role as FSOC chairperson, but it does not include information on FSOC's goals or how it will measure FSOC's progress in achieving them.

OFR, which is not independently subject to GPRA, also received limited discussion in Treasury's 2012-2015 strategic plan. Specifically, the plan notes only that Treasury's Office of Domestic Finance supports OFR and that OFR was created by the Dodd-Frank Act. Similar to other entities within the Treasury such as the Bureau of the Public Debt and the Internal Revenue Service, and consistent with leading practices for new organizations, OFR is undertaking an independent strategic planning and performance management effort. OFR issued a strategic framework in March 2012 to cover fiscal years 2012-2014. In the strategic framework OFR lists five strategic goals, including supporting FSOC through the secure provision of high-quality financial data and by conducting the analyses needed to monitor threats to financial stability; developing and promoting data-related standards and best practices; and providing the public with key data and analyses while protecting sensitive information. The framework also highlights a number of objectives under those goals and lays out implementation priorities for the first year covered by the document, fiscal year 2012. The framework also notes the importance of transparency and that OFR is subject to oversight from the Treasury Office of the Inspector General (OIG) and GAO, which have both exercised that authority during OFR's first two years, and that the Dodd-Frank Act requires that the OFR Director testify before Congress annually on OFR's activities. However, OFR acknowledges within its framework document, that it does not yet have certain other key elements of performance management in place including linking programmatic, human resources, and budgetary decision making to its strategic goals and developing a performance measurement system. The framework identifies establishing these elements of a performance management system among its fiscal 2012 priorities. OFR officials told us that they have begun to link its budget and human resources to strategic goals and that the human resources plan to be submitted to Congress in September 2012 and the fiscal year 2014 budget submission to be issued in 2013 will reflect these linkages.[26] They added that at the time they issued the framework, they were not in a position to include performance measures, as the agency was not sufficiently established. However, they plan to include performance measures in their fiscal year 2014 budget submission. In June 2012, the Treasury OIG issued a report on the progress OFR had made in developing an implementation plan that lays out how it will stand up all of its operations and also noted the need to develop performance measures.[27] Without developing and publishing such performance measures, neither the agency nor the public can determine whether OFR's expenditures and activities are most effectively aimed at accomplishing its mission.

In the absence of a strategic plan, FSOC's annual reports serve as a key accountability document. An FSOC policy official said that at this time he views FSOC's annual reports as its strategic planning document. FSOC staff noted that its annual reports provide Congress and the public with a report on FSOC's activities, its views on potential emerging threats to U.S. financial stability, and recommendations to enhance the integrity, efficiency, competitiveness, and stability of U.S. financial markets. They note further that the council's chairperson is required to testify annually before Congress on the report, which serves as an accountability mechanism. When discussing accountability, FSOC members have noted the importance of the statement contained in the front of the reports (and signed by each member) that FSOC is taking reasonable steps to ensure financial stability and mitigate systemic risk.[28] FSOC members have also acknowledged the need to follow up on recommendations, and FSOC staff noted that recommendations will be monitored by FSOC as a whole. However, the annual reports do not effectively communicate how FSOC will be held accountable for the actions identified. For example, the annual reports list multiple recommendations that FSOC plans to monitor over time, but do not specify how they will conduct that monitoring. For example, who is going to monitor or implement the recommendations and the recommendations themselves is often vague or unclear, and no time frames are specified. More specifically, in the 2011 Annual Report some recommendations identified relevant parties only as "market participants" or "regulators" but did not consistently identify the targets of the recommendation or designate parties responsible for monitoring or implementing them. Another recommendation only discusses Dodd-Frank Act reforms, while several others express support for certain aspects of international coordination on financial reforms. In the 2012 Annual Report, FSOC adds some specificity to these recommendations, such as recommending an expeditious implementation of the Dodd-Frank Act. In the 2012 Annual Report, FSOC also more clearly identifies recommendations starting each one with "the council recommends," but it still does not consistently designate an FSOC member or members to monitor or implement the recommendations nor does it establish time frames for certain actions such as reporting to the council on the status of the recommendation. Treasury officials noted that the Dodd-Frank Act did not give the chairperson or council authority to require that independent regulators take action or impose time frames on them. However, they noted that some recommendations in the 2012 Annual Report were made to specific agencies and put greater stress on more immediate action than others. For example, the report emphasized the importance of a recommendation to SEC to take action to address money market fund risks by saying that wholesale short-term funding markets are a critical component of a well-functioning financial system, and FSOC continues to be focused on structural vulnerabilities in money market funds that could disrupt these markets. Enhancing FSOC's accountability could lead to more effective oversight and public confidence in financial institutions and markets.

In addition, while FSOC releases minutes from its meetings, as required by its bylaws, it does not keep detailed records of deliberations or discussions that take place at these meetings or at the committee level. While no specific level of detail is required for FSOC minutes, the limited documentation of their discussions makes it difficult to assess FSOC's performance. Another deliberative body, the Federal Reserve's Federal Open Market Committee, keeps transcripts of its meetings and voluntarily releases these transcripts to the public after 5 years. Releasing the transcripts after a period of time should allow the members of the committee to talk freely and provides documentation that can be used to assess the entity's performance and monitor their decision making process.

FSOC and OFR Have Taken Steps to Build Mechanisms to Identify Potential Threats to Financial Stability, but More Work Is Needed to Realize This Goal

FSOC has taken steps to meet its statutory responsibilities related to identifying risks and potential emerging threats to U.S. financial stability, but has not yet developed comprehensive and systematic mechanisms to realize these goals. These steps include setting up the Systemic Risk Committee that is responsible for systemic risk monitoring and plays a key role in reviewing sources of systemic risk. Potential threats to financial stability are also discussed at FSOC meetings; for example, FSOC officials noted that a teleconference was convened to discuss MF Global. The Systemic Risk Committee generally meets every 2 weeks and is co-chaired by the Commodity Futures and Trading Commission (CFTC), FDIC, the Federal Reserve, and SEC. The committee is operating under draft procedures in which member agency staff suggest risks or threats that, in their view, may benefit from interagency coordination.[29] In December 2011, FSOC members' staff provided 40 suggestions, which FSOC policy staff grouped into categories for discussions at the committee's monthly meetings. According to FSOC policy staff, if there is agreement that an issue would warrant further examination, an agency is assigned to develop the issue, including identifying vulnerabilities in the financial system. When the committee determines the issue is sufficiently developed, it presents the issue to the Deputies Committee. Sending some issues to the Deputies Committee sooner than others does not imply that the committee attaches greater importance to the issue but only that enough analysis has been completed to allow it to move forward. According to the draft procedures, if issues are elevated beyond the Deputies Committee to FSOC members, agencies may respond with a variety of actions, including enhanced monitoring, additional analysis, the development of potential policy responses, or the implementation of a particular policy response.[30]

OFR participates in the Systemic Risk Committee and is building capacity to monitor the financial system for threats to financial stability. OFR has developed the Financial Stability Monitor, a collection of metrics and indicators related to financial stability that is to be continuously updated, according to OFR and Treasury officials. According to these officials, OFR began sharing the Financial Stability Monitor with the Systemic Risk Committee and FSOC member agency staff in February 2012. OFR is assessing options for analyzing risks to financial stability and produced a working paper in collaboration with outside researchers, published in January 2012, to survey existing approaches.[31] In addition, OFR and FSOC sponsored a conference in December 2011 to discuss data and technology issues and analytical approaches for assessing threats to financial stability.[32]

Although they are building some mechanisms to identify risks to the U.S. financial system, FSOC and OFR have not yet developed and implemented systematic and comprehensive mechanisms for identifying and monitoring these risks. A systematic approach would incorporate both rigorous methods—such as quantitative indicators and models—to assess vulnerabilities of the financial sector, as well as qualitative inputs to account for any shortcomings of the quantitative models or gaps in available data. A comprehensive approach would better ensure that all relevant aspects of the financial system are considered and analyzed. The Systemic Risk Committee procedures may facilitate analysis of risks that could benefit from interagency discussions and responses, but these procedures may not help to identify new risks or threats that FSOC member agencies have not already identified on their own. Without a more systematic approach and comprehensive information, FSOC member agencies, on their own, may not be well positioned to judge which potential threats will benefit from interagency discussions. FSOC and OFR could improve their efforts to identify risks and threats by collecting and sharing a common set of financial indicators.[33] Systematic collection, analysis, and sharing of financial indicators of key risk factors such as leverage, liquidity, concentrations, underwriting standards, collateral quality, and delinquencies should provide insight into vulnerabilities affecting particular types of financial intermediaries or reveal patterns occurring across the financial system. OFR, through a mechanism such as the Financial Stability Monitor, could play a role in collecting, analyzing, and reporting on these indicators. A senior OFR official told us that this was the ultimate intent of the Financial Stability Monitor. A sample of the Financial Stability Monitor that we reviewed included, among other topics, some indicators of leverage and liquidity that were based on data from the federal banking agencies and purchased databases.

Many analytical tools have been developed by researchers or are in use by international bodies to assess the risk of a financial crisis or identify vulnerabilities in the financial system. Some of these tools—such as early warning models—can be useful to assess the overall level of risk in the financial system, while others, such as system-wide stress testing, could be helpful in identifying new vulnerabilities and interconnections (see figure 3). In general, these tools are methods of integrating large volumes of financial information to generate specific insights about financial stability. Experts we spoke with were generally supportive of developing and using such tools for monitoring risks to financial stability and also emphasized the importance of using multiple tools. These tools, which all have useful features as well as shortcomings, may complement each other, and exploring a variety of tools will provide insight into which ones will be the most effective. According to FSOC policy staff, FSOC has not formally considered whether to develop early warning models or conduct system-wide stress tests. OFR staff said they are evaluating a range of metrics and methods that had been proposed for measuring and analyzing financial markets and systems and are in the early stages of developing network maps and other tools to assess financial stability. OFR evaluated 11 measures against a series of crises over time and reported on some of these efforts in its 2012 Annual Report.[34] In addition, OFR has a statutory responsibility to report on stress testing, and OFR officials told us that they interpreted that responsibility as contributing to the development and evaluation of quantitative tools that are used in stress tests, improving the data used in stress tests, and helping to advance the state-of-the-art in stress test methodologies. As such, OFR's survey of systemic risk approaches described several stress testing models and the OFR Annual Report noted that methodologies will need to advance to expose vulnerabilities in the financial system as a whole. OFR would support FSOC in evaluating system-wide stress tests, according to OFR officials.

Limited Public Information Hinders Understanding of FSOC's and OFR's Activities and Progress

Although FSOC and OFR have adopted communication methods to provide information to the public and Congress on their activities, some of their methods could be strengthened. For example, both entities have web pages on Treasury's website. FSOC's web pages include minutes of the council's meetings, annual reports, frequently-asked-questions, and information on FSOC rulemakings. OFR has also posted key documents on its web pages, including its annual report, strategic framework, and updates on recent developments, such as the status of the legal entity identifier.[35] OFR's first annual report discusses its activities and agenda for the next year, and its approach to researching financial stability as well as current threats. The annual report also covers other topics including data gaps in the areas of leverage, liquidity, and interconnectedness as well as the benefits of data standards. Treasury officials also provided us with examples of emails they have sent to congressional committees on key FSOC or OFR products or actions, such as the designation of nonbank financial companies, and described the wide range of correspondence they respond to on congressional inquiries involving both entities.

Early warning models 	Early warning models have been widely studied and their relative merits are well understood.[a] Researchers have found that these models would have provided useful signals of financial stress before the 2007-2009 financial crisis.[b] Early warning models typically combine a number of financial indicators and determine which combination would have best predicted previous financial crises. The optimal combination is then used to forecast the likelihood of future financial crises. Some models emphasize a small number of high-level financial indicators, such as the total supply of credit in the economy, bank capital and liquidity, and measures of asset prices. Other models integrate information from a larger number of financial indicators, including the money supply, exchange rates, and measures of the balance of international trade, as well as the supply of credit and asset prices.
Financial stability mapping 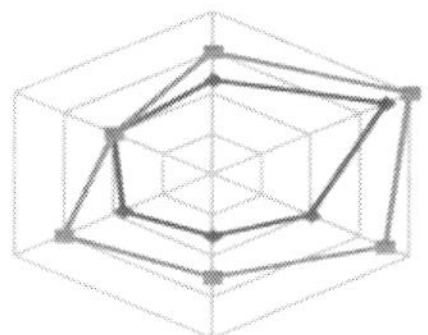	Financial stability mapping is another technique for representing aspects of the degree of risk in the financial system. The goal of this approach is to provide a visual representation of risk that can more easily reveal patterns. Researchers at the European Central Bank (ECB) and International Monetary Fund (IMF) have developed financial stability mapping approaches.[c] The financial stability map developed by ECB researchers—not yet in use by ECB—is designed to monitor vulnerabilities by locating a country in the financial stability cycle: precrisis, crisis, postcrisis, or tranquil. The approach at IMF, known as the Global Financial Stability Map, has been in use since 2007. IMF's map is intended to provide a graphical representation of IMF's assessment of financial stability based on six factors: macroeconomic risks, emerging market risks, credit risks, market and liquidity risks, risk appetite (the willingness of investors to take on risk), and monetary and financial conditions. In assessments by the respective researchers, both IMF approach and the approach developed by ECB researchers provided some early warning indications of financial stress.
System-wide stress testing 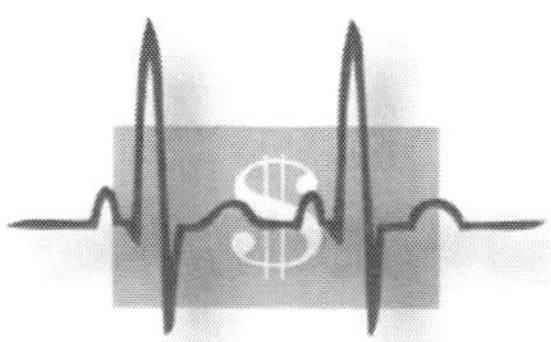	One approach that would take advantage of the varying supervisory responsibilities of FSOC member agencies is system-wide stress testing, or stress testing that is designed to evaluate the broader financial system and understand linkages between the different markets and institutions. Stress testing is a technique for assessing the resilience of financial institutions or systems to extreme events. In contrast to the Federal Reserve's stress testing of large bank holding companies, a system-wide approach would stress different types of financial intermediaries (e.g., banks, money market funds, and insurance companies) to understand not just how intermediaries would fare in stress scenarios, but also how their responses would affect other financial intermediaries. Linkages between types of financial intermediaries were found in retrospect to have been critically important during the 2007-2009 financial crisis, and several groups, including OFR, have emphasized the importance of assessing interconnections between institutions when performing stress tests.[d] Nevertheless, these groups have also acknowledged the analytical and practical challenges associated with analyzing linkages among financial institutions. Alternatively, "top down" or "macro" stress tests rely less on institution-specific information and more on estimated relationships between the financial system and the economy.

Source: GAO analysis of academic literature; Art Explosion (images).

[a] See, for example, Marco Lo Duca and Tuomas Peltonen, *Macro-Financial Vulnerabilities and Future Financial Stress: Assessing Systemic Risks and Predicting Systemic Events*, ECB Working Paper 1311 (Frankfurt, Germany: March 2011); E. Philip Davis and

Dilruba Karim, "Could Early Warning Systems Have Helped to Predict the Sub-Prime Crisis?" *National Institute Economic Review* 206 (October 2008); *International Monetary Fund, The IMF-FSB Early Warning Exercise: Design and Methodological Toolkit* (Washington, D.C.: September 2010). See also Andrew K. Rose and Mark M. Spiegel, *Cross-Country Causes and Consequences of the 2008 Crisis: Early Warning*, NBER Working Paper 1537 (Cambridge, Ma.: September 2009) for some concerns about early warning approaches.

[b] See Ray Barrell, E. Philip Davis, Dilruba Karim, and Iana Liadze, "Bank Regulation, Property Prices and Early Warning Systems for Banking Crises in OECD Countries," *Journal of Banking and Finance* 34 (2010); Claudio Borio and Mathias Drehmann, "Assessing the Risk of Banking Crises -Revisited," BIS Quarterly Review (March 2009).

[c] See Peter Sarlin and Tuomas Peltonen, *Mapping the State of Financial Stability*, ECB Working Paper 1382 (Frankfurt: September 2011); Peter Dattels and others, *Can You Map Global Financial Stability?*, IMF Working Paper WP/10/145 (Washington, D.C.: June 2010).

[d] See Pew Financial Reform Project, *Standards for Financial Stress Tests* (Washington, D.C.: June 2011); Basel Committee on Banking Supervision, *Principles for Sound Stress Testing Practices and Supervision* (Basel, Switzerland: May 2009); Institute of International Finance, *Macroprudential Oversight: An Industry Perspective* (Washington, D.C.: July 2011. The Bank of England also recently completed work on a model featuring interconnections in the banking industry to examine the potential impact of various stress scenarios on the UK financial system. See David Aikman and others, *Funding Liquidity Risk in a Quantitative Model of Systemic Stability*, Bank of England Working Paper 372 (London: June 2009).

Figure 3. Selected Tools for Monitoring Risks to Financial Stability.

FSOC releases the minutes of its meetings. However, the minutes describe general agenda items for the meetings and information on the presenters for each agenda item and lack additional detail even when the information being discussed is not likely to be market sensitive or limit the quality of deliberations. For example, the meeting minutes for October 11, 2011, show that several presentations were given during an executive session, including one on money market reform updates. The minutes provide the names of those who gave the money market presentation and note that updates were provided on actions taken since the last presentation on the topic. However, the minutes lack any content of the actual presentation or discussion.[36] Specifically, the minutes say the following.

"Money Market Fund Reform Update

"The Chairperson then turned to the agenda item regarding an update on money market fund reform and called on Robert Plaze, Associate Director, Division of Investment Management, SEC, Matthew Eichner, Associate Director, Division of Research and Statistics, Federal Reserve, Matthew Rutherford, Deputy Assistant Secretary for Federal Finance, Treasury, to make the presentation. The individuals listed above provided the presentation which included a review of the actions taken since the last presentation regarding money market fund reform to the Council, the reform options under consideration, and next steps.

The members of the Council asked questions about the presentation."

In addition, in our review of meeting minutes for meetings held from October 2010 through December 2011, we found that minutes from more recent meetings generally have less detail than those from earlier ones. As a result, the public receives little information about FSOC's activities and deliberations, which limits the public's understanding of its activities. More recently, however, FSOC provided additional transparency on a key decision—its 2012 Annual Report provides extensive information on the designation of FMUs as systemically important, including the names of the designated entities and a discussion of the reasons for their designation.

FSOC policy officials acknowledged that the issue of transparency is challenging. They recognized the need for transparency but also noted that certain information is protected from disclosure under various statutes and cannot be released. FSOC staff also noted the need to balance the desire for transparency with the need to provide an environment that allows for open discussion and deliberation of issues and policy options. As we have previously reported, transparency is a key feature of accountability even when there is a need to safeguard certain sensitive information to protect the marketplace.[37] In addition, the Freedom of Information Act (FOIA) recognizes that deliberative processes also need to be safeguarded so that decision makers can have meaningful discussions and certain information that FSOC considers, such as that collected by bank supervisors, is prohibited from public disclosure. However, similar bodies, such as the Federal Open Market Committee and the Interim Policy Committee in the UK—an entity that has a similar role to FSOC's—publishes minutes that provide greater detail. Although the Federal Open Market Committee makes certain announcements on the day it meets, after a 3-week delay, it publishes its more detailed meeting minutes, which usually include a detailed discussion of developments in financial markets and the economy, committee member views, and an explanation of committee policy actions. In addition, as noted earlier in this report, 5 years after its meetings, the Federal Open Market Committee voluntarily releases transcriptions of those meetings. The minutes of the Interim Policy Committee in the UK provide information on what the committee discussed and an update on the health of the economy, including threats to financial stability.

Additionally, neither FSOC nor OFR has taken full advantage of modern communication tools to communicate information about their activities or progress. While using a search engine, such as Google, identifies web pages for both entities on Treasury's website, the pages are not easy to locate from Treasury's homepage nor are the sites user friendly. For example, the FSOC and OFR web pages are in a section of Treasury's website called Initiatives and are further embedded under a section titled Wall Street Reform. While FSOC does post the dates and times of its meetings on its web page, this information is in a link at the bottom of the page rather than being prominently displayed. In addition, FSOC does not have an online service that regularly alerts interested parties to changes to its web pages or upcoming meetings. Further, one member of FSOC noted that FSOC relies on emails to members and staff rather than having a portal where members can access needed information more easily and securely.

OFR's web pages have been evolving over time especially during July and August of 2012, but it could further improve its website. For example, we had noted in June 2012 that OFR did not consistently display agency testimonies in the same place; in August 2012, OFR rectified these omissions. Similarly, in March 2012, OFR told us that the Treasury daily blog provided information about OFR activities, but timely notices relevant to OFR have not regularly appeared there. For example, many of the recent developments related to global approval of the legal entity identifier, which OFR cites as a major endeavor, have not appeared in a timely manner. In July 2012, OFR added an online service to its own web pages to inform those who register that updates have been made to the site, but there was a delay in having the feature work consistently. However, OFR has not posted some information that would show the progress the agency is making in standing up its operations, such as its organization chart including the names of its top managers. In comparison, the Consumer Finance Protection Bureau, which was also created by the Dodd-Frank Act, has for some time had its own domain name, an easily identifiable website that includes an organization chart, and online services that provide regular updates to interested parties.

Some industry representatives, academics, and former government officials have questioned the progress that the new entities have made. Some industry representatives with whom we spoke said that they did not believe that FSOC and OFR had met their expectations for streamlining regulatory requirements (e.g., responding to data requests), improving coordination on new regulations, or providing new information on systemic risks. Some members of FSOC and their staffs said that they learned a great deal from working on and reading the 2011 Annual Report; however, some industry representatives with whom we spoke said that they did not find that report useful. Among other concerns, industry representatives told us that the report did not contain any new information on systemic risks or the status of Dodd-Frank act reforms. In addition, a group of former government officials, academics, and industry representatives convened the Systemic Risk Council in June 2012 to address concerns that they said stemmed, in part, from the lack of progress made by the members of FSOC and OFR. They said that their concern increased each day that the implementation of systemic reform languished. The Systemic Risk Council also noted that it was essential for FSOC to provide clear and transparent explanations of regulatory reforms in a way that the general public could understand. Communicating more effectively with groups critical to their missions and the public could improve FSOC's and OFR's ability to effectively and efficiently achieve their missions.

FSOC AND OFR HAVE TAKEN STEPS TO COLLABORATE BUT COULD ENHANCE THEIR EFFORTS

The Dodd-Frank Act recognizes the importance of collaboration and requires FSOC and OFR to collaborate on various activities. Effectively building mechanisms to identify risks and potential emerging threats to U.S. financial stability will also require FSOC and OFR to collaborate with a number of internal and external stakeholders. To date, FSOC and OFR have taken steps to promote collaboration; however, they could enhance collaboration by more fully incorporating some key elements of effective collaboration. Taking full advantage of opportunities to work with stakeholders could strengthen FSOC's and OFR's ability to carry out their missions. For example, in testifying about the need to coordinate agency rulemakings, FSOC's Chairperson noted the importance of coordinating both domestically and internationally to prevent risks from migrating to regulatory gaps—as they did before the 2007-2009 financial crisis—and to reduce U.S. vulnerability to another financial crisis. In addition, effective collaboration could eliminate unnecessary duplication for both the industry and regulators.

The Dodd-Frank Act Recognizes the Importance of Collaboration to FSOC's and OFR's Missions

Recognizing the importance of collaboration to FSOC's and OFR's missions, the Dodd-Frank Act assigns specific collaboration duties and responsibilities to these new entities. Title I of the act directs FSOC to facilitate information sharing and coordination among its member agencies and other federal and state agencies regarding domestic financial services policy development, rulemaking, examinations, reporting requirements, and enforcement actions.[38] In addition, FSOC must consult with the primary financial regulatory agency, if any, before designating a nonbank financial company for supervision by the Federal Reserve.

The Dodd-Frank Act also encourages collaboration between FSOC and external stakeholders, especially state regulators and international entities. For example, it permits FSOC to appoint technical and professional advisory committees which could include industry representatives and academics as well as state regulators that may be useful in carrying out the council's functions. The act eases the creation of committees by generally exempting them—and FSOC—from the Federal Advisory Committee Act (FACA), which requires agencies to adhere to a formalized process to ensure that committees are objective and accessible to the public.[39] The act also directs the FSOC chairperson, in consultation with FSOC members, to regularly consult with financial regulatory entities and other appropriate organizations of foreign governments or international organizations on matters relating to systemic risk to the international financial system. Further, when designating foreign nonbank financial companies for supervision by the Federal Reserve, FSOC must consult with appropriate foreign regulatory authorities, to the extent appropriate.

The Dodd-Frank Act also specifies a number of duties for OFR that require collaboration with FSOC members and others. In particular, OFR must collect data on behalf of FSOC, provide the data to FSOC and member agencies, and standardize data collection among the agencies.[40] These activities require collaboration not only with FSOC member agencies but also with commercial data providers, publicly available data sources, and the financial industry. In addition, like FSOC, OFR can appoint technical and professional advisory committees to help leverage necessary resources, but these are not exempt from FACA.

FSOC and OFR Have Taken Steps to Promote Collaboration

FSOC and OFR have taken steps to enhance collaboration among FSOC members and member agencies and with external stakeholders. Members' staffs stated that FSOC's organizational and committee structures help support collaboration both on a formal and informal basis. Through these committees, staff from member agencies said they have developed good working relationships with staff from other agencies. Prior to FSOC, two means of collaborating were the President's Working Group on Financial Markets and the Federal Financial Institutions Examination Council.[41] Members' staffs noted that communication within FSOC had been broader and deeper than in either of those forums because staff from more agencies participate in FSOC at various levels. For example, staff said that various FSOC committees and working groups have allowed staff to develop contacts at other agencies with whom they can consult and share information on a variety of topics. In addition, staff said that through FSOC they had become acquainted with others having different expertise and have had the opportunity to share their views and experience with others. For example, the independent insurance member and his staff noted that they had used FSOC as a forum to provide information on insurance companies' use of money market funds, which may differ from the more common retail fund mechanisms.

Through the committee structure, FSOC members' staffs also noted that agencies had leveraged their joint expertise and resources to carry out FSOC's statutory responsibilities, including rulemakings. For example, an ad hoc interagency lawyers group was formed shortly after the passage of the Dodd-Frank Act to provide regular input into the rulemaking process. The standing committees also provide input on rulemakings dealing with issues within their areas of expertise. In addition, throughout the rulemaking processes the Deputies Committee was briefed regularly, especially on issues that could not be resolved in other committees or working groups. The deputies kept their respective FSOC members informed throughout the rulemakings.

We discussed with Treasury staff the FSOC chairperson's consultations with financial regulatory entities and other appropriate organizations of foreign governments or international organizations on matters relating to systemic risk to the international financial system. Treasury staff noted that the FSOC chairperson, who is also the Secretary of the Treasury, has regular contact with foreign officials and shares information from these interactions with other U.S. regulators at FSOC meetings. They said that they have monitored these activities and believe that FSOC is complying with the Dodd-Frank requirement.

Further, OFR has taken some actions to collaborate by leveraging the expertise of external stakeholders and coordinating U.S. activities internationally. In particular, FSOC and OFR held a joint conference in December 2011 to discuss data and technology issues and analytical approaches for assessing threats to financial stability. The conference included attendees from the financial regulatory community, academia, public interest groups, and the financial services industry. OFR has also initiated a working paper series in which OFR researchers have collaborated with outside academics to catalog systemic risk monitoring systems and ways to improve risk management at financial institutions. In addition, OFR has invited experts on various aspects of financial stability to give seminars to OFR and FSOC policy staff. OFR has also announced plans to create the Financial Research Advisory Committee to solicit advice, recommendations, analysis, and information from academics, researchers, industry leaders, government officials, and experts in the fields of data and technology. Applications were due in April 2012, and in August 2012 OFR officials said that the list of applicants was in the final stage of review. OFR officials also noted that they play a key role on FSOC's Data Committee, which supports coordination of and consultation on issues related to FSOC data collection and sharing.

In addition, OFR is working to standardize data reporting systems among FSOC member agencies. OFR officials noted that the agency had begun a three-stage process to assemble an inventory of data collected by FSOC member agencies as a first step toward standardizing data, reducing duplication, and eventually lowering costs for industry and regulators. The three stages examine data (1) purchased by the agencies, (2) collected through regulatory activities, and (3) derived by the agencies from data they purchased or collected. An OFR official said that the first phase was complete but had taken longer than initially envisioned because of the complexities of the project including agencies' use of different terminology for the same databases. For instance, the official noted that it had been difficult to create an effective survey instrument to capture the data purchased by the agencies, because the survey instrument had to capture the different terminology used by the various agencies. OFR officials said that they expected the process to allow them to determine when multiple agencies used the same data, identify data gaps more effectively, and seek potential savings in data acquisition. For example, they have been able to negotiate contracts that provide the small office of the independent insurance member of FSOC with access to expensive private databases. OFR officials said that OFR is also working with FSOC member agencies through FSOC's Data Committee to address differences in existing security classification systems and support efficient, secure data-sharing efforts given the statutory responsibilities agencies have to ensure the confidentiality of certain data. Many industry representatives with whom we spoke said that this project could help relieve regulatory burdens by standardizing data-reporting systems and reducing duplication, noting that currently multiple agencies ask for the same data but in different formats or at different times.

Moreover, OFR has collaborated with industry, foreign government entities, and international bodies to create a legal entity identifier, which OFR describes as an emerging global standard that will enable regulators and companies around the world to quickly and accurately identify parties to financial transactions. Building on earlier industry and interagency efforts and on CFTC's and SEC's responses to mandates on data standards, OFR led U.S. government efforts to promote global adoption of the identifier. Within the expert group appointed by the Financial Stability Board to develop recommendations for the Group of 20 (G20) countries regarding the identifier, OFR led the U.S. consultative group, and OFR staffers have been leading singly or jointly the development of a governance framework and operating protocols.[42] The Financial Stability Board endorsed the expert group's recommendations in May 2012. In June 2012, the G20 endorsed the proposal, which includes a target for implementing a legal entity identifier system globally, with some allowance for variation across countries, by March 2013. OFR continues to serve as the vice-chair for the Americas on the group charged with implementing the identifier.

FSOC Could Enhance Collaboration by Incorporating Key Practices

While the previous examples show the progress FSOC and OFR have made in terms of promoting collaboration, other examples suggest that additional actions are needed. In our prior work, we have identified practices that agencies can use to enhance and sustain their collaborative efforts. These include identifying and addressing needs by leveraging resources, agreeing on roles and responsibilities, and establishing mutually reinforcing or joint strategies.[43] The examples below highlight areas in which FSOC's collaboration efforts could be enhanced by more fully reflecting these principles.

Leveraging resources. FSOC has not taken advantage of opportunities to leverage resources through its authority to appoint technical and professional advisory committees. In addition to state regulators and council members, the Dodd-Frank Act specifies that such committees could include other persons. Such persons could be those from the industry and academics. Industry representatives have commented on the benefits of having industry input through such a committee, but, to date, FSOC has not established such committees. Moreover, the ability of FSOC members to leverage expertise varies. For example, while FSOC members from federal regulatory agencies are able to draw on staff from across their agencies, the independent insurance member and state representatives have limited support structures. The state representatives are limited by the number of support staff that have been allowed to sign required confidentiality agreements and this may limit these members' access to certain regulatory expertise. The representative of state insurance regulators noted that he must rely solely on his limited department staff and a small group of staff from the National Association of Insurance Commissioners that have been detailed to his department and have signed the confidentiality agreement to support his FSOC activities, including committee representation. In a letter to the FSOC Chairperson, the National Association of Insurance Commissioners and the State Insurance Representative that is a member of FSOC, stated that the State Insurance Representative had been prohibited from discussing or seeking guidance from other relevant state regulators even on a confidential basis. Subsequent to this letter, FSOC issued an "operational interpretation" of the MOU on the treatment of nonpublic information. This interpretation states in part that the MOU does not prevent an FSOC member from consulting or discussing with anyone FSOC proposals, rules or other matters provided that the member does not (1) disclose specified types of confidential information; (2) attribute nonpublic proposals, rules or other matters to FSOC or any of its members or (3) disclose their views on such matters.

Similarly, the representative of the state banking regulators is supported by four staff from the Conference of State Bank Supervisors and the representative of the state securities regulators by two staff from the North American Securities Administrators Association. The state banking member's staff noted that Treasury had worked with the state members to secure their assistance, and that the State Banking Supervisor generally had adequate staff support. However, they did note that they think the process limited access to other state banking supervisors with specialized expertise. For example, they noted that they might want to consult with New York banking staff on international issues before FSOC, but confidentiality restrictions limit them to sharing information on FSOC matters only with the member, his state banking staff, and others who have signed a confidentiality agreement. In addition, the FSOC state insurance representative and his staff told us that because of the confidentiality restrictions, they had limited their discussions at International Association of Insurance Supervisors meetings, because they thought they could not speak to issues being discussed within FSOC.

Agreeing on roles and responsibilities. As noted earlier, FSOC is tasked with monitoring the financial services marketplace to identify potential threats to U.S. financial stability, and OFR must develop and maintain metrics and reporting systems for risks to U.S. financial stability as well as monitor, investigate, and report on changes in system-wide risk levels. These responsibilities overlap somewhat, but this overlap is not unexpected given OFR's primary mission of supporting FSOC. FSOC and OFR staff cited their statutory responsibilities for monitoring risks to U.S. financial stability as the reason that both organizations are pursuing efforts in this arena. FSOC and OFR staff also noted that OFR participates on the Systemic Risk Committee, allowing for some coordination of efforts. The Dodd-Frank Act defines certain responsibilities for FSOC and OFR, but, the lack of clear responsibility for implementation can lead to duplication, confusion, and gaps in their efforts. This risk is further compounded by the fact that many FSOC member agencies have risk analysis and data collection functions associated with their supervisory responsibilities. Some of these functions are explicitly focused on risks to financial stability, and some member agencies have created their own programs to examine these risks. For example, in 2010 the Federal Reserve created an Office of Financial Stability Policy and Research to identify and analyze potential threats to financial stability. FDIC, SEC, and the Federal Housing Finance Agency have also created offices in recent years to monitor risks to financial stability originating in their regulated markets. To the extent that these programs provide unique information to FSOC, they will be contributing to the overall effort. However, if not properly coordinated, these separate efforts could be duplicative, resulting in wasted time and resources.

Establishing reinforcing or joint strategies. To achieve a common outcome, collaborating agencies need to establish strategies that work in concert with those of their partners or that are joint in nature. Such strategies help in aligning activities, core processes, and resources to reach a common outcome. In this area, FSOC has taken actions to better coordinate members' rulemakings. In October 2010, it issued an integrated implementation road map for the Dodd-Frank Act that included a list of the rules regulators were required to promulgate, provided a time line for those rulemakings, and identified the agencies responsible for each rulemaking. FSOC has also developed a consultation framework for the agencies involved in rulemakings where consultation is required by the Dodd-Frank Act. The framework establishes time frames for coordinating three tasks: initial interagency meetings, circulation of term sheets for interagency comments, and circulation of proposed rules for interagency comments. In a November 2011 report, we noted that although FSOC's road map and consultation framework were a positive development in facilitating coordination, they had limited usefulness.[44] For example, the consultation framework does not provide, nor according to FSOC staff is it intended to provide, any specifics about staff responsibilities or processes to facilitate coordination. For example, it does not mention the extent to which interagency coordination is required or what happens when rulemakings conflict with or duplicate each other. As a result, we recommended that FSOC work with the federal financial regulatory agencies to establish formal coordination policies that would clarify issues such as the timing of coordination, the process for soliciting and addressing comments, and FSOC's role in facilitating coordination.[45] To date, FSOC has not implemented this recommendation. Industry representatives with whom we spoke also questioned why FSOC could not play a greater role in coordinating member agencies' rulemaking efforts. As an example of how coordination could be improved, representatives noted that FSOC's rule and interpretive guidance on designating nonbank financial companies for Federal Reserve supervision was finalized before the Federal Reserve had issued a rule laying out the requirements for determining whether a company would fall within the statutory definition of a financial company.[46] FSOC and Federal Reserve staff said that after the timetable was set for the FSOC rule, the Federal Reserve decided that it needed to clarify some issues with its rulemaking, creating the anomaly of having a process for designating financial companies before the requirements for meeting the definition of a financial company had been adequately identified. The Secretary of the Treasury, FSOC's Chairperson has noted in testimony before the Congress that he does not have the power to force FSOC members to collaborate on rulemakings.

FSOC Has Issued Rules and Reports but Processes May Not Ensure That Ongoing Activities Have the Intended Results

The Dodd-Frank Act requires FSOC to consult on a number of regulatory agency rulemakings, but it gave FSOC a few responsibilities that have led it to issue its own rules. These responsibilities include the authority to designate FMUs as systemically important and nonbank financial companies for supervision by the Federal Reserve under its enhanced prudential standards and to reevaluate the latter designations annually. While individual designations are not made by rule, in an effort to be more transparent, FSOC has issued rulemakings explaining the processes and criteria it will follow in making the individual designations. However, FSOC is not required to and has not developed a separate process to assess the overall impact of these designations including whether they are having the intended result of improving U.S. financial stability. The Dodd-Frank Act also mandated that FSOC issue a number of reports during its first two years, and FSOC has issued these by the mandated due dates. Most of these were one-time reports; however, FSOC is also mandated to report annually on a number of items, including potential emerging threats to financial stability. Both the 2011 and 2012 Annual Reports identify a number of threats, but they do not use a systematic forward-looking process for doing so. As a result, the reports may not be providing the public and Congress with the best information for guiding their decisions relative to these threats.

FSOC Has Issued Rules on Processes for Designating Certain Financial Entities for Additional Supervision and the Freedom of Information Act

The Dodd-Frank Act provided FSOC with the authority to designate FMUs as systemically important. FMUs are to be considered systemically important if FSOC determines that the failure of an FMU or a disruption in its functioning could threaten U.S. financial stability. Similarly, the Dodd-Frank Act provided FSOC with the authority to designate nonbank financial companies for supervision by the Federal Reserve under its enhanced prudential standards.[47] The act stipulates that FSOC may designate these companies for Federal Reserve supervision if material financial distress at that company, or the nature, scope, size, scale, concentration, interconnectedness, or mix of the activities of the company, could pose a threat to U.S. financial stability. The Federal Reserve has not issued final rules on its enhanced prudential standards, but other final rules that will apply to designated nonbank financial companies have been issued. These rules include a rule on resolution plans or "living wills," jointly issued by the Federal Reserve and FDIC that will require designated nonbank financial companies to prepare resolution plans and a rule, issued by the Treasury, which establishes an assessment schedule for the Financial Research Fund—the fund that finances OFR and FSOC under the Dodd-Frank Act.[48]

FSOC issued final rules on the processes FSOC intends to use for designating FMUs as systemically important and nonbank financial companies for Federal Reserve supervision in July 2011 and April 2012, respectively. In accordance with the Dodd-Frank Act, both rules specify that two-thirds of FSOC's voting members, including the chairperson, must vote to designate FMUs and nonbank financial companies. Each rule, with any accompanying interpretive guidance, also outlines a multistage process that FSOC intends to follow in designating these entities, including a process for designated entities to request an FSOC hearing before the designation becomes final. In its 2012 Annual Report, FSOC reported that it had designated eight FMUs as systemically important. In contrast, FSOC has not yet designated any nonbank financial companies.

In April 2012, FSOC also issued a rule implementing the Freedom of Information Act (FOIA).[49] The Dodd-Frank Act states that FOIA, including its exceptions from disclosure, applies to any information submitted to FSOC or OFR under title 1 of the act. It further states that FSOC, OFR, and member agencies are to maintain the confidentiality of such information if that confidentiality is protected from public disclosure by federal or state law.[50] While FOIA would apply with or without a rule, FSOC issued a rule setting out the procedures for requesting access to information contained in its records.

FSOC Generally Followed Similar Processes for Rules That Required Limited Regulatory Analysis

According to Treasury officials and staff, FSOC's rulemaking authority is narrow compared to that of the member agencies. The Dodd-Frank Act requires that those agencies issue a large number of rules, while it assigns few authorities to FSOC that may lead to rulemakings. Although FSOC does not have extensive rulemaking authority or written policies and procedures, its rulemakings followed a general process. For each rule, FSOC published a notice of proposed rulemaking in the Federal Register before issuing a final rule and included a time period for public comments (see table 1). Treasury staff noted that FSOC was not required to issue the various rulemakings but went through this process to provide greater public transparency of its processes. According to FSOC and Treasury officials, officials and staff from Treasury's Office of General Counsel led the rule-drafting process, with officials and staff from Treasury's Office of Domestic Finance, including the FSOC policy staff, and members' staffs contributing significantly to the drafting of the designations rules. The processes relied on various groups and mechanisms to get feedback from officials and FSOC members' staffs including standing committees and ad hoc working groups. The Deputies Committee was briefed regularly throughout the process, especially on issues that could not be resolved in other committees or working groups. Deputies kept their respective FSOC members informed throughout the rulemakings, and the members received all of the rule-making notices and final rules at least 48 hours before they were to be voted on at FSOC meetings. FSOC members voted unanimously to issue all of the rule-making notices and final rules before they were published in the Federal Register.

Although the process for the rulemakings followed a general pattern, the number of notices, the time between the initial notice and the final rule, and the number of comments varied considerably across rules. Generally, these differences reflected differences in priorities and the potential impact of each rule. For example, FSOC and some member agency officials attributed the longer lapse between receiving comments on the notice for implementing FOIA and issuing the final rule to the relatively low priority attached to completing this rule. Officials told us that the rule remained a relatively low priority because FSOC had not yet begun gathering information under the FMU and nonbank financial company designation rules. In contrast, the long gap between the receipt of comments on the first notice of proposed rulemaking for the nonbank financial company rule and the issuance of the final rule reflects the complexities of developing a rule that encompasses a broad range of industry segments and the potential impact on them.

Table 1. FSOC Rules Issued between July 21, 2010 and July 20, 2012

Title	Issuance date	Due date for comments	Number of comments	Effective date
Authority to Designate Financial Market Utilities as Systemically Important				
Advance Notice of Proposed Rule-making (NPR)	December 21, 2010	January 20, 2011	12	
NPR	March 28, 2011	May 27, 2011	15	
Final Rule	July 27, 2011	n/a	N/A	August 26, 2011
Authority to Require Supervision and Regulation of Certain Nonbank Financial Companies				
Advance NPR	October 6, 2010	November 5, 2010	50	
NPR	January 26, 2011	February 25, 2011	35	
Second NPR	October 18, 2011	December 19, 2011	41	
Final rule	April 11, 2012	n/a	N/A	May 11, 2012
Implementation of the Freedom of Information Act				
NPR	March 28, 2011	May 27, 2011	9	
Final rule	April 11, 2012	n/a	N/A	May 11, 2012

Source: GAO summary of information from the Federal Register.

Note: n/a stands for not applicable.

During the gap between the first and second notices of proposed rulemaking for designating nonbank financial companies, FSOC and OFR staff developed information to support a set of thresholds for determining which nonbank financial companies would pass from the first stage of the designation process to the second. The thresholds, which were included in the interpretive guidance that accompanies the second notice, use publicly available information so that the first stage would be transparent. Financial companies have to meet a size threshold of $50 billion in assets and one of five other thresholds, including measures of leverage and debt. The thresholds generally reflect staff calculations. Staff generally calculated thresholds by placing the threshold at an interval above the mean that considers the dispersion of the data from the mean. Staff also tested to see whether certain companies that experienced material distress during the 2007-2009 financial crisis would have been captured by the threshold. The data used were generally either data on the 19 largest bank holding companies or nonbank financial companies in 2007 and 2008.

FSOC is subject to laws and executive orders that require certain regulatory analyses as part of its rule-making processes. These include the Paperwork Reduction Act and the Regulatory Flexibility Act, as well as Executive Orders 12866 and 13563 (Executive Orders). Among other things, the Paperwork Reduction Act requires agencies to justify any collection of information from the public and to estimate the time and expense required to comply with the paperwork requirements in the rule. The Regulatory Flexibility Act requires federal agencies to assess the impact of their regulation on small entities and consider regulatory alternatives to lessen any regulatory burden. The Executive Orders require FSOC to assess the economic effects of economically significant rules, including the quantitative and qualitative benefits and costs of those regulations.[51]

However, FSOC was required to consider costs and benefits only as they relate to the Paperwork Reduction Act for the FMU and nonbank financial company rulemakings. As a result, these rules contain estimates of the time needed to comply with paperwork requirements. FSOC estimates the annual reporting burden for the FMU rule at 500 hours and for the nonbank financial company rule at 1,000 hours. The FMU rule does not include an estimate of the cost of the projected hours; the cost for the hours imposed by the nonbank financial company rule is estimated at $450,000 a year. FSOC concluded that small entities were unlikely to be designated as posing a risk to U.S. financial stability, and thus an analysis of the rules designating FMU and nonbank financial companies' impact on small entities was not required. In addition,

FSOC did not conduct a benefit-cost analysis for the rules designating FMUs or nonbank financial companies because the Office of Management and Budget determined that these rules were not economically significant. Treasury officials noted that the rule did not impose substantive requirements on specific entities, but only laid out the process by which they could become subject to other rules and regulations. In addition, FSOC member staff noted that costs and benefits of the designation were not among the factors that the Dodd-Frank Act directs FSOC to consider when making a designation.

FSOC Has Not Set up Processes to Assess Whether Designating FMUs and Nonbank Financial Companies Will Have the Intended Impact

Designating FMUs and nonbank financial companies was intended to address certain risks to financial stability posed by these entities. The designations, however, have the potential to confer certain benefits and costs on the wider economy and individual entities being designated. Examples of potential benefits and costs of subjecting FMUs and nonbank financial companies to heightened supervision include the following:

Economy-wide benefits. The Dodd-Frank Act provides FSOC with the authority to designate nonbank financial companies because Congress believed that these companies could threaten U.S. financial stability. Subjecting companies to enhanced supervision may contribute to financial stability.

Individual benefits. Some research has shown that certain large, interconnected financial institutions considered too big to fail may have higher credit rating agency ratings and lower borrowing costs than would otherwise be warranted. As a result, designated nonbank financial companies that are not already treated as too big to fail by rating agencies or markets could see their borrowing costs fall.[52]

Economy-wide costs. Industry representatives have noted that regulations such as minimum capital requirements that may be imposed on designated entities have the potential to reduce the availability of credit and slow economic growth.

Individual costs. Some of those who commented on the nonbank financial company rule noted that being designated would impose a significant regulatory burden on the designated companies. Designated nonbank financial companies will be subject to supervision similar to that for large bank holding companies, required to prepare resolution plans, and assessed fees to fund the operation of OFR and FSOC. However, the impact of these Dodd-Frank Act provisions on designated nonbank financial companies will not be known until the rules are applied. Designated FMUs could also experience increased costs.

The Dodd-Frank Act requires FSOC to rescind any designation if the institution no longer meets the FMU or nonbank financial company standards and specifically requires FSOC to reevaluate nonbank financial company designations at least annually. The final rule for designating certain nonbank financial companies for enhanced supervision says FSOC will notify a nonbank financial company prior to an annual reevaluation and provide the company up for review with an opportunity to submit written materials to contest the designation. However, the rule also notes that reevaluations will focus on material changes since a previous review rather than a full replication of the original designation process. In the interpretive guidance for the nonbank financial company designations, FSOC says that it also intends to review the appropriateness of both the stage one thresholds and the levels of the thresholds that are specified in dollars as needed, but at least every five years, and to adjust the thresholds and levels as it may deem advisable. However, FSOC has not set up processes to conduct a comprehensive assessment of the overall impact of designations.

Doing a comprehensive analysis to assess whether designations are having their intended impact of providing greater financial stability and the extent of any other impacts will be challenging. Namely, establishing a baseline from which to evaluate the overall impact of various rules will likely be complex because the impact of being designated will depend on the application of a number of rules being written by multiple independent regulatory agencies and issued over a span of time.[53] For example, rules the CFTC, Federal Reserve, and SEC are writing will help determine the impact of being designated a systemically important FMU. Similarly, the impact of being designated a nonbank financial company will be influenced by the rule the Federal Reserve is writing, to implement enhanced prudential standards; the Federal Reserve and FDIC rule on resolution planning; and Treasury's rule on assessments to fund FSOC and OFR. Moreover, not all of these agencies are required to conduct cost-benefit analyses that might be useful in establishing a baseline for ongoing evaluation. For example, neither the Federal Reserve nor FDIC are subject to the Executive Orders that require an economic analysis of the costs and benefits of certain rules. Furthermore, while some regulatory agencies may conduct periodic retrospective reviews of their rules, these reviews tend to focus only on the rules issued by their agency.

FSOC is uniquely positioned to address this challenge. FSOC is responsible for designating FMUs and nonbank financial companies, and its member agencies are responsible for writing the rules that will impact these designated entities. Moreover, FSOC can rely on OFR for some data collection and analysis. However, FSOC members would need to collaborate on such an assessment, because FSOC policy and OFR staff, who are Treasury employees, may not have access to all of the needed information. In addition, collaboration is needed because, according to Treasury officials, it would be inappropriate for FSOC staff to review rules drafted by independent agencies unless those agencies agreed to participate in the comprehensive assessment. Without such an assessment, decision makers may not have the information they will need to determine whether designating new entities for enhanced supervision and other requirements and restrictions is addressing a perceived gap in the regulatory system and improving the stability of the financial system or whether policy changes should be considered.

FSOC Has Issued Mandated Reports, but Does Not Have Sufficient Processes for Identifying or Prioritizing Emerging Threats

As table 2 shows, the Dodd-Frank Act mandated that FSOC issue a number of reports, including five one-time studies and ongoing annual reports.[54] Although some of the timelines were short—two of the studies had to be issued in 6 months—and the subject matter difficult, FSOC met all of its mandated report timelines and generally strove to address the specific items in the mandate. For example, the mandated studies generally began with a discussion of the mandate itself and the extent to which the report could address certain questions. The 2011 Annual Report also generally addressed the subjects in the mandate, including identifying emerging threats to financial stability of the nation and recommendations to enhance the integrity, efficiency, competitiveness, and stability of U.S. financial markets; promote market discipline; and maintain investor confidence.

The processes that FSOC used to issue all of the reports were generally similar to those used for rulemakings. Treasury officials led activities related to issuing the studies, except that the Federal Reserve staff led activities for and was the author of the study on concentration limits. For the annual reports, FSOC brought on detailees from Federal Reserve District Banks to lead the process. For all of the reports, the process relied on ad hoc working groups of member staff to provide input. FSOC also relied on the Deputies Committee to help manage the process and keep FSOC members informed of key decisions. The members voted unanimously to issue all of the reports.

Table 2. Reports Mandated by the Dodd-Frank Act and Issued by FSOC from July 21, 2010 to July 20, 2012

Report title Studies	Issuance date	Number of public comments	Number of recommendations
Studies			
Study & Recommendations on Prohibitions on Proprietary Trading & Certain Relationships with Hedge Funds & Private Equity Funds	January 2011	8,000[a]	10
Study & Recommendations Regarding Concentration Limits on Large Financial Companies	January 2011	6	3
Report to the Congress on Secured Creditor Haircuts	July 2011	n/a	0
Report to the Congress on Prompt Corrective Action	December 2011	n/a	0
Report to Congress on Study of a Contingent Capital Requirement for Certain Nonbank Financial Companies and Bank Holding Companies	July 2012	n/a	1
Annual reports			
FSOC 2011 Annual Report	July 2011	n/a	14
FSOC 2012 Annual Report	July 2012	n/a	29

Source: GAO summary of information from FSOC. Note: n/a stands for not applicable.

[a] This number includes 6,550 similar letters that FSOC describes as essentially the same letter with different signatures.

FSOC's annual reporting process is an ongoing responsibility which, in the absence of a strategic plan, functions as its major strategic planning document and method for communicating with Congress and the public, especially regarding potential emerging threats to U.S. financial stability. FSOC's early annual reports provide extensive information about the current economy and complex issues, such as high-frequency trading and the MF Global bankruptcy. In addition, the reports provide extensive discussions of current known threats such as those associated with money market funds and the European sovereign-debt crisis and makes some recommendations to address them. However, FSOC has not developed a structure that supports having a systematic or comprehensive process for identifying potential emerging threats. The process for identifying these threats is similar, in some ways, to that used by the Systemic Risk Committee. Members' staffs, including some members of the Systemic Risk Committee, identify specific threats for consideration. As a result, new threats that members or staff have not already identified may not be included.

In addition, the lack of a systematic process for identifying potential emerging threats leads to potential inconsistencies in identifying such threats. For instance, certain potential threats related to U.S. debt, are not in the 2011 Annual Report. Instead this report has a conflicting message on the danger the U.S. debt poses to financial stability.[55] The project leader of the 2011 Annual Report said that the report did not include the U.S. debt as an emerging threat because of issues of balance and the inappropriateness of FSOC speculating on the credit risk associated with U.S. Treasury securities. However, the 2012 Annual Report identifies the U.S. debt as a potential threat, but does not explain what has changed since the 2011 report.[56] Similarly, the 2011 report includes several threats associated with possible unintended consequences of new regulations being written to implement the Dodd-Frank Act, but the 2012 report does not include these threats. The 2012 report does include a framework for identifying potential emerging threats, but, this framework, which separates threats into shocks to the system and vulnerabilities in the system that would exacerbate shocks, is not equivalent to the kind of systematic analysis that would help determine both the likelihood of a threat and its likely severity. Without a systematic process that consistently identifies threats Congress and the public might believe that a threat has grown in importance or been addressed when that is not the case.

Similarly, neither the 2011 or 2012 annual reports use a systematic forward-looking approach to identify potentially emerging threats. As a result, they comingle threats that emerged during the 2007-2009 crisis, current threats, and potentially emerging threats. Although the 2012 report notes that structural vulnerabilities that contributed to the 2007-2009 financial crisis associated with mortgage-backed securities backed by subprime mortgage debt built up over an 8-year period, the report does not use a systematic mechanism for identifying similar kinds of asset build-ups or other market changes that might signal a potential emerging threat. Rather the report often identifies risks, such as those associated with the European sovereign-debt crisis or money market funds, which are ongoing or have previously been identified, although it acknowledges that these events may change in the future in ways that are not currently known. The 2012 report does include at least one area that could be considered potentially emerging—threats associated with having a low interest rate environment. Specifically it notes threats associated with market participants taking on more risk to increase their earnings but says it does not see evidence of this now. Threats that emerged during the crisis or those that are currently evident likely require different and perhaps more immediate responses than those that are potentially emerging. The comingling of well-known risks with risks that are developing, but less well-known, reduces the ability of policymakers and market participants to develop effective and timely responses for the latter.

Further, the FSOC process for identifying threats limits its ability to explicitly prioritize the large number of threats identified. The 2011 report includes over 30 threats without explicitly specifying which are most important. The 2012 report also includes a lengthy list of threats without explicit prioritization. In contrast, other entities, such as the International Monetary Fund and European Central Bank, issue reports that explicitly prioritize potentially significant threats. Treasury and FSOC officials and staff noted that FSOC's Annual Reports have a different purpose and implicitly prioritize the threats in the recommendations sections of the reports. For example, they noted that the recommendation for money market funds—a threat included in the potentially emerging section— notes that the vulnerabilities associated with money market funds are a particular focus of FSOC. They contrasted this recommendation with other recommendations, such as those related to the low interest rate environment that notes that regulators and industry should adopt certain practices to help monitor the situation. However, the lack of a systematic process that explicitly prioritizes potential emerging threats leaves policymakers without the information they need to focus on or allocate scarce resources to the most important threats.

CONCLUSIONS

The 2007-2009 financial crisis highlighted how the nation's fragmented regulatory structure was not equipped to monitor and address risks across the financial system, nor did it have the needed information to facilitate that oversight. To address this weakness, Congress created FSOC and OFR to improve the U.S. government's ability to identify and respond to future threats to financial stability. This is a daunting task, and one that is made more challenging as FSOC and OFR must concurrently stand-up organizations and establish a sense of collective accountability among the independent regulators and other members.

Successfully implementing their mandates will require FSOC members to actively work together and with external stakeholders. Appropriate accountability and transparency mechanisms also need to be established to determine whether FSOC and OFR are effective and to ensure that the public and Congress have sufficient information to hold the entities accountable for results. Over the last 2 years, FSOC and OFR have made progress on these fronts. Staff from FSOC member agencies told us that the level of collaboration and communication among the agencies has increased since the creation of FSOC and that such collaboration has resulted in more information sharing and diverse perspectives being considered. OFR has also made contributions to international efforts, such as coordinating U.S. input on the Legal Entity Identifier, to enhance governments' abilities to track financial activity.

While FSOC and OFR have made some progress, continued efforts to improve the entities' accountability, transparency, and collaboration are needed. As we have seen, for example:

- OFR issued a strategic framework in March 2012 that covered the period fiscal years 2012-2014. This represented an important step for the new agency in adopting leading practices in performance management. The framework identifies OFR's strategic goals, highlights a number of objectives under those goals, and lays out implementation priorities for the first year covered by the document. However, as OFR acknowledges, the framework does not include key elements of a performance management system, such as linking programmatic, human resources, and budgetary decision making to its strategic goals and developing performance measures. OFR expects to communicate progress on these key elements when it provides a new human resources plan to Congress in September 2012 and in its fiscal year 2014 budget submission. Moving forward, transforming its framework into a comprehensive strategic planning and performance management system can provide the agency with a long-term vision and allow others to hold it accountable which will be critical for OFR.
- The critical role of monitoring threats to financial stability and responding to emerging threats also needs to be further developed. Potential threats to financial stability are discussed at FSOC meetings and FSOC has established a Systemic Risk Committee to facilitate coordination among members' staffs, including member agencies that often have their own groups devoted to risk analysis. In addition, OFR is evaluating a variety of potential tools for assessing financial stability and studying methods to improve stress tests. Collectively,

these efforts remain incomplete. The approach of the Systemic Risk Committee can help FSOC analyze known risks but does not take full advantage of FSOC member agency resources to identify new threats to the financial system. Without more systematic and comprehensive mechanisms, including comprehensive sharing of key financial risk indicators, risks to financial stability may develop in the system without being recognized.

- FSOC and OFR have attempted to be transparent with some of their decision making and activities. FSOC, for instance, posts the minutes from its meetings and other key documents on Treasury's website, and it provided insight into its designations processes through multiple rulemakings and comment periods as well as by providing additional information on the designation of FMUs in its 2012 Annual Report. OFR also posted some information on Treasury's website and provided information on a wide range of OFR activities and research in its first annual report issued in July 2012. As we found, however, both FSOC and OFR could be more transparent. For example, FSOC's minutes contain limited details about the council's discussion and the amount of detail included in the minutes has declined over time. While some information discussed must remain confidential given potential market sensitivities, legal restrictions on sharing certain information, and the need for members to deliberate, striving to be as transparent as possible given the potential impact of some of its decisions on institutions and markets is important for FSOC. FSOC's and OFR's limited transparency has caused some former government officials, industry representatives, and academics to question whether they are making progress. Continued efforts to increase transparency will allow the public and Congress to better understand FSOC's and OFR's decision making, activities, and progress.
- FSOC and OFR have taken some steps to encourage collaboration, such as FSOC setting up standing committees composed of members' staffs and OFR beginning to establish a professional and technical advisory committee. However, more needs to be done to promote collaboration—both among FSOC members and between FSOC and external stakeholders. For example, FSOC has not yet set up advisory committees, and OFR and FSOC have not yet clarified their responsibility for implementing statutory requirements for monitoring and reporting on threats to U.S. financial stability, including the

responsibilities of member agencies. More fully incorporating the key practices for successful collaboration, including agreeing on roles and responsibilities and establishing reinforcing or joint strategies, could make FSOC's and OFR's existing collaboration efforts more effective. Effective collaboration could eliminate unnecessary duplication for both the industry and regulators. In addition, it could help to fill regulatory gaps so that risks would not migrate to unregulated markets or countries as they did prior to the 2007-2009 financial crisis.

- One of FSOC's most significant actions, to date, has been finalizing its rules for designating FMUs and nonbank financial companies for additional oversight. The Congress intended that the enhanced supervision of those entities designated would lead to greater financial stability. In addition, the designations will likely have other important ramifications for the designated entities—which will become subject to a number of other rules and regulations—and potentially the nation's economy. While FSOC must periodically reevaluate the nonbank financial company designations and intends to review the thresholds for stage one of the nonbank financial company process at least every 5 years, it is not required to conduct a comprehensive assessment to determine whether the designations are having their intended impact of improved financial stability as well as other consequences. Establishing a baseline and developing a framework to comprehensively assess the impact of the designations will be difficult because of the number of independent regulators involved. But, without such an analysis, Congress, the affected institutions, the public, and FSOC cannot determine whether the designations and associated oversight is actually helping to improve financial stability.
- While FSOC's annual reports identify a number of potential emerging threats to the nation's financial stability, they do not use a systematic forward-looking approach to identify such threats. Thus, some threats may not be identified consistently or at all. Threats such as those associated with the long term U.S. debt appear in FSOC's 2012 Annual Report but had not appeared in FSOC's 2011 Annual Report and there was no explanation for the change. The reports are also not forward-looking in that many of the identified threats, such as those associated with money market funds or the European debt crisis, will not potentially emerge but rather emerged during the 2007-2009 financial crisis or more recently. Finally, the reports do not explicitly

prioritize the emerging threats relying instead on a careful reading of the recommendations to determine which are critical. In addition, these recommendations do not consistently identify which member agency or agencies are recommended for implementing or monitoring the council's recommendations. The lack of this information makes determining which well-recognized threats require immediate action, which potential emerging threats are most likely to have severe outcomes, and how best for decision makers to address the differing threats. Finally, it does not allow Congress to hold FSOC accountable for identifying potential emerging threats or implementing the recommendations.

Whether FSOC and OFR fundamentally change the way the federal government monitors threats to financial stability remains an open question. This is due, in part, to the newness of the entities, as both continue to develop needed management structures. But limits to FSOC's and OFR's transparency also contribute to questions about their effectiveness. Addressing the issues we have identified will help FSOC and OFR shed more light on their decision making and activities and allow Congress to hold them accountable for results. Moreover, addressing these issues can help FSOC and OFR to further promote collaboration among FSOC's members and with external stakeholders, which is critical to their ability to achieve their missions. If they do not succeed in achieving their missions the financial system will remain vulnerable to large or multiple shocks that could result in large losses in asset values, higher unemployment, and slower economic growth associated with previous financial crises.

Recommendations for Executive Action

While FSOC and OFR have made progress in establishing their operations and approaches for monitoring threats to financial stability, developing accountability and transparency mechanisms, and enhancing collaboration among the financial regulatory agencies, these efforts could be strengthened. Therefore, we are recommending that the Secretary of the Treasury take 10 actions—some in his capacity as the Chairperson of FSOC, in consultation with FSOC members, and in his leadership role for OFR, which does not yet have a confirmed director.

We recommend that FSOC and OFR clarify responsibility for implementing requirements to monitor threats to financial stability across FSOC and OFR, including FSOC members and member agencies, to better ensure that the monitoring and analysis of the financial system are comprehensive and not unnecessarily duplicative.

As FSOC continues to develop approaches for monitoring threats to financial stability, we recommend that FSOC develop an approach that includes systematic sharing of key financial risk indicators across FSOC members and member agencies to assist in identifying potential threats for further monitoring or analysis.

To improve the transparency of FSOC and OFR operations, we recommend that FSOC and OFR each develop a communication strategy to improve communications with the public. The strategy could include using technology more effectively to communicate, such as having fully developed websites, sending regular notices to interested parties, and developing methods to communicate with the public.

To support the growth of OFR into a viable and sustainable entity, we recommend that OFR build on its strategic framework by further developing its strategic planning and performance management system so that it links its activities to its goals and uses publicly available performance measures to measure its progress.

To strengthen accountability and collaboration in FSOC's decision making, we recommend that FSOC take the following six actions:

- Keep detailed records (for example, detailed minutes or transcripts) of closed door sessions of principals meetings and to the extent possible make them publicly available after an amount of time has passed sufficient to avoid the release of market-sensitive information or information that would limit deliberations.
- Establish formal collaboration and coordination policies that clarify issues such as when collaboration or coordination should occur and what role FSOC should play in facilitating that coordination.
- More fully incorporate key practices for successful collaboration that we have previously identified. Internally, this could include working with agencies to rationalize schedules for rulemakings and conducting collaborative system-wide stress testing. Externally, this could include using professional and technical advisors including state regulators, industry experts, and academics.

- Establish a collaborative and comprehensive framework for assessing the impact of its decisions for designating FMUs and nonbank financial companies on the wider economy and those entities. This framework should include assessing the effects of subjecting designated FMUs and nonbank financial companies to new regulatory standards, requirements, and restrictions; establishing a baseline from which to measure the effects; and documenting the approach.
- Develop more systematic forward-looking approaches for reporting on potential emerging threats to financial stability in annual reports. Such an approach should provide methodological insight into why certain threats to financial stability are included or excluded over time, separate current or past threats from those that are potentially emerging, and prioritize the latter.
- Make recommendations in the annual report more specific by identifying which FSOC member agency or agencies, as appropriate, are recommended to monitor or implement such actions within specified time frames.

AGENCY COMMENTS AND OUR EVALUATION

We provided a draft of this report to the Secretary of the Treasury—as the Chairperson of FSOC and in his leadership role for OFR—for review and comment. Treasury's Under Secretary for Domestic Finance, on behalf of the Chairperson of FSOC, provided written comments. Treasury also provided technical comments on the draft report, which we incorporated as appropriate. Treasury solicited views from staff of the FSOC members and member agencies on the draft report and reflected these views in the comments provided to us.

In their written comments, Treasury emphasizes the progress that FSOC and OFR have made since their creation. For example, Treasury highlights FSOC's work in issuing a final rule and guidance relating to the designation of nonbank financial companies for enhanced supervision and designating eight systemically important FMUs that will be subject to enhanced risk management standards. Treasury also highlights OFR's progress in building its organization and analytical capabilities, including the launch of OFR's working paper and seminar series for research on financial stability and risk management. Treasury also outlines efforts FSOC and OFR have taken to promote transparency and accountability, including testifying before Congress, responding to requests for information from oversight bodies, conducting voluntary rulemakings, or making information available on websites. In addition, Treasury also emphasizes that the progress that each entity has made to date should be viewed with the understanding that both entities are relatively new. Nevertheless, Treasury recognizes that more work remains. In the report, we also describe FSOC's and OFR's efforts, to date, in fulfilling their statutory responsibilities and efforts to promote accountability and transparency. The report also notes that both entities were established in 2010.

In its letter, Treasury states that officials will carefully consider the report's findings and recommendations. Treasury further notes that the Secretary, in his role as Chairperson, will share the recommendations with the Council for their review and consideration. Treasury also offers initial reactions to several of our recommendations. First, regarding our recommendation that FSOC and OFR should clarify their responsibilities for monitoring threats to financial stability, Treasury states that there is no existing confusion or overlap of responsibilities. Furthermore, Treasury states that both organizations are working together to pursue their distinct, but complementary, statutory missions, and cites OFR's efforts to develop the Financial Stability Monitor, a collection of indicators related to financial stability that Treasury expects will be shared with FSOC members. In the report, we point out that Congress gave both FSOC and OFR responsibilities for monitoring systemic risk—responsibilities that both entities must fulfill. We also highlight that multiple FSOC members, such as the Federal Reserve, also have ongoing efforts to monitor threats to financial stability. The report does not suggest that any overlap between these efforts currently exist. Rather, the report recommends that these similar statutory responsibilities and ongoing efforts should be clarified and carefully coordinated. While Treasury notes that no confusion or overlap currently exists, our past work has shown that without clearly delineating and coordinating roles and responsibilities there can be duplication of efforts, confusion, and regulatory gaps. In addition, the report notes the importance of a systematic and comprehensive approach to identifying threats to financial stability. While OFR's Financial Stability Monitor could be a vehicle for sharing key financial risk indicators, it does not yet reflect a comprehensive interagency effort to collect and share indicators related to financial stability.

Second, Treasury states that it expects FSOC will consider the effects on the financial system resulting from designation in its periodic assessments in response to our recommendation that FSOC develop a framework for assessing the impact of its decisions for designating FMUs and nonbank financial companies on the wider economy and those entities. The Dodd-Frank Act requires FSOC to periodically review the designation of nonbank financial companies, and FSOC intends to periodically review FMU designations. However, FSOC is not currently required to examine the potential economic impact of the designations. In our report, we detail the types of benefits and costs that individually designated firms, as well as the economy at large, may experience as a result of the designations. Given the potential magnitude of these benefits and costs of the designations, a comprehensive assessment of their impact is warranted.

Third, Treasury agrees that OFR should implement a robust strategic planning and performance management system as the office grows.

Treasury describes OFR's past and ongoing efforts on this front, highlighting, for example, OFR's March 2012 strategic framework. In the report, we note that the strategic framework was an important first step for OFR, and we also describe OFR's efforts to develop an independent strategic planning and performance system, including performance measures, and time lines for publicly releasing this information. We acknowledge OFR's efforts in continuing to develop the elements required for a strategic plan and performance management system and will review this information when it is publicly released.

Finally, Treasury notes our recommendation regarding OFR's communications strategy is consistent with the office's ongoing efforts. The letter describes OFR's efforts to improve communication and notes that FSOC's website is being redesigned to improve usability and navigation. The report also recognizes OFR's recent efforts to improve their communication methods, such as the recent capability OFR added to its website enabling the public to sign up for email alerts on recent OFR activities.

A. Nicole Clowers
Director
Financial Markets and Community Investment

Appendix I. Objectives, Scope, and Methodology

The objectives of this report are to examine the Financial Stability Oversight Council's (FSOC) and Office of Financial Research's (OFR) (1) challenges in fulfilling their missions; (2) efforts in establishing management structures and mechanisms to carry out their missions and attain their goals;

and (3) activities for supporting collaboration among members and external stakeholders, including international bodies and regulators; as well as (4) FSOC's processes used to issue rules and reports.

To identify and examine any challenges faced by FSOC and OFR, we reviewed our prior reports on regulatory reform and the financial crisis. We also reviewed statements of government officials, members of Congress, and academic experts. In addition, we interviewed FSOC policy staff and support staff of FSOC members, including staff and officials at member regulatory agencies. At OFR, we interviewed senior officials and some staff members.

To examine FSOC's and OFR's efforts in establishing management structures and mechanisms to carry out their missions, we reviewed the Dodd-Frank Wall Street Reform and Consumer Protection Act (Dodd-Frank Act), FSOC's bylaws and organizational structure (including its committee structure), and OFR's strategic framework. We reviewed minutes from FSOC's principals' meetings (i.e., the meetings with the designated FSOC members, many of whom are heads of regulatory agencies), and we reviewed the minutes from the Federal Reserve's Federal Open Markets Committee and the United Kingdom Interim Policy Committee meetings for comparison purposes. We also examined the entities' fiscal years 2012 and 2013 budget requests, budgetary and staffing data, and congressional testimonies. We assessed the reliability of OFR's staffing data by comparing the data provided with information contained in the President's budget for fiscal year 2013 and FSOC testimony in April 2011. We also tested the data for consistency over time. We determined the data were sufficiently reliable for our purposes. To understand the steps OFR is taking to protect the sensitive data it collects, we interviewed OFR officials with knowledge of data security efforts, reviewed the OFR strategic framework, and reviewed Congressional testimony provided by OFR. In addition, we reviewed the Department of the Treasury Inspector General reports on the stand-up of OFR and the Consumer Financial Protection Bureau. We used criteria from *Standards for Internal Control in the Federal Government*, our past work on the stand-up of federal entities, such as the Millennium Challenge Corporation, and managing for results to evaluate FSOC and OFR management structures and mechanisms, including their need for strategic planning and performance measures. We reviewed selected academic literature on tools used or proposed to identify potential threats to financial stability by entities that write financial stability reports, including the European Central Bank, Bank of England, and International Monetary Fund, and others, including the Institute for International Finance and Pew Financial Reform Project. We also attended FSOC's and OFR's December 2011 conference entitled *Macroprudential Toolkit: Measurement and Analysis*. We interviewed some FSOC members; officials from FSOC federal regulatory agencies whose heads are members of FSOC (member agencies); support staff of other FSOC members; FSOC, OFR, and other Treasury officials and staff; and academics who have published research related to systemic risk and worked on financial stability reports.[57] We also coordinated with the Treasury Office of Inspector General and the Council of Inspectors General on Financial Oversight regarding their ongoing audits of FSOC and OFR.

To determine how FSOC and OFR support collaboration, we reviewed our criteria for effective collaboration and compared it to FSOC and OFR policies and practices. We analyzed the Dodd-Frank Act requirements for collaboration, FSOC's transparency policy, hearing procedures, Dodd-Frank Act integrated implementation roadmap, and memorandum of understanding on information sharing. We also reviewed FSOC's products, such as the 2011 Annual Report, and interviewed FSOC staff and officials from FSOC member agencies and some FSOC member support staff to determine how FSOC members collaborate, including how they participate in the drafting of the products. To determine how collaboration practices among and between domestic and international financial regulators have changed since the creation of FSOC, we reviewed FSOC, OFR, and some member agencies' congressional testimony and reports from international bodies, such as the Financial Stability Board. Finally, we interviewed representatives from industry trade groups, government officials in the United Kingdom, and experts from the European Union. We selected individuals from the United Kingdom and European Union because those entities have experience working with U.S. federal financial regulators and councils designed to enhance financial stability.

To examine the process and procedures FSOC and OFR used in issuing products, we analyzed FSOC rules or reports issued before July 2012 including FSOC's 2011 and 2012 Annual Reports. We analyzed the content of public comments on three proposed rules to examine how FSOC addressed them in the final rules. We also reviewed documentation on the process FSOC staff used to document and address comments from member agencies on the 2011 Annual Report. In addition, we examined the analyses and other materials provided to FSOC members prior to their meetings, including material to be presented at the meetings dating from October 2010 through December 2011 and selected documents thereafter through March 2012. We interviewed officials from FSOC member agencies, FSOC and OFR policy staff who had responsibility for contributing to the products within our scope, academics who have published research related to systemic risk, and industry or trade groups who submitted comments on a number of FSOC rules and reports. Finally, using testimonial and documentary evidence, we compared FSOC's rulemaking process, rules, and reports with key practices identified in our prior work on rulemaking and standard economic practice, where applicable.[58]

We conducted this performance audit from November 2011 to September 2012 in accordance with generally accepted government auditing standards. Those standards require that we plan and perform the audit to obtain sufficient, appropriate evidence to provide a reasonable basis for our findings and conclusions based on our audit objectives. We believe that the evidence obtained provides a reasonable basis for our findings and conclusions based on our audit objectives.

APPENDIX II. STANDING COMMITTEES OF THE FINANCIAL STABILITY OVERSIGHT COUNCIL

FSOC has established seven standing committees. The committees and brief descriptions are listed below.

- *Deputies Committee*: Coordinates and oversees the work of the interagency staff committees. The members of the Deputies Committee are senior officials from each of the member agencies. Treasury chairs this committee.
- *Systemic Risk Committee*: Includes senior staff and reports to the Deputies Committee. The committee is accountable for systemic risk monitoring and will play a role in prioritizing the review of sources of systemic risk and guiding the work of staff and the systemic risk subcommittees. Treasury chairs this committee. It has two subcommittees.
    - *Institutions Subcommittee*: Focuses on identifying and analyzing issues that affect financial institutions in the medium and longer term. It also attempts to identify structural issues within financial institutions that could threaten financial stability, such as trends in leverage or funding structure, new products, or exposures to particular risks. The Board of Governors of the Federal Reserve

(Federal Reserve) and the Federal Deposit Insurance Corporation (FDIC) chair this subcommittee.

- *Markets Subcommittee*: This subcommittee focuses on identifying and analyzing issues that affect financial markets in the medium and longer term, including structural issues within financial markets that could threaten financial stability, such as trends in volatility or liquidity, market structure, or asset valuations. The Commodity Futures Trading Commission (CFTC) and Securities and Exchange Commission (SEC) chair this committee.

- *Designation of Nonbank Financial Companies Committee*: Supports FSOC in considering, making, and reviewing designations of nonbank financial companies to be supervised by the Federal Reserve. The Federal Reserve and FDIC chair this committee.
- *Designation of Financial Market Utilities Committee*: Supports FSOC in considering, making, and reviewing designations of financial market utilities and payment, clearing, and settlement activities. The Federal Reserve, SEC, and CFTC chair this committee.
- *Heightened Prudential Standards Committee*: Supports FSOC in making recommendations for heightened prudential standards with respect to designated nonbank financial companies and large, interconnected bank holding companies, and with respect to other financial activities and practices that could impact financial stability. This committee also supports FSOC's authorities for monitoring regulatory developments, facilitating information sharing, recommending supervisory priorities and principles, and identifying gaps in regulation that could pose risks. The Federal Reserve and the Office of the Comptroller of the Currency chair this committee.
- *Orderly Liquidation Committee*: Supports any FSOC recommendations on resolution plan requirements, consideration of filed resolution plans, and consideration of FDIC and Federal Reserve proposed orders to require divestiture; and consults with FSOC on rulemakings to implement the Title II orderly liquidation authority. FDIC and Treasury chair this committee.
- *Data Committee*: Supports FSOC coordination of, and consultation on, agency rulemakings on data collection, and seeks to minimize duplication of data gathering operations. The committee supports a coordinated approach to information sharing and provides direction to, and requests data from, the Office of Financial Research (OFR).

Additionally, the committee works with OFR on data standardization efforts. Treasury chairs this committee.

End Notes

[1] Pub. L. No. 111-203, 124 Stat. 1376 (2010).

[2] The provisions of the Dodd-Frank Act dealing with FSOC are contained primarily in subtitle A of title I, §§ 111-123, codified at 12 U.S.C. §§ 5321-5333, and title VIII, codified at 12 U.S.C. §§ 5461-5472. The following sections of this report describe FSOC's specific functions in detail.

[3] The provisions dealing with OFR are contained primarily in subtitle B of title I, §§ 151-156, codified at 12 U.S.C. §§ 5341-5346.

[4] The Council of Inspectors General on Financial Oversight, which was created by the Dodd-Frank Act, is made up of the inspectors general of eight federal agencies—the Federal Reserve, Commodity Futures Trading Commission (CFTC), Department of Housing and Urban Development, Treasury, Federal Deposit Insurance Corporation (FDIC), Federal Housing Finance Agency, National Credit Union Administration, and Securities and Exchange Commission (SEC)—and the Special Inspector General of the Troubled Asset Relief Program.

[5] GAO, *Results-Oriented Government: Practices That Can Help Enhance and Sustain Collaboration among Federal Agencies*, GAO-06-15 (Washington, D.C.: Oct. 21, 2005).

[6] See for example, GAO, *Financial Regulation: Modernization of the Financial Services Regulatory System*, GAO/T-GGD-95-121 (Washington, D.C.: Mar. 15, 1995); *Long-Term Capital Management: Regulators Need to Focus Greater Attention on Systemic Risk*, GAO/GGD-00-3 (Washington, D.C.: Oct. 29, 1999); *Financial Regulation: Industry Changes Prompt Need to Reconsider U.S. Regulatory Structure*, GAO-05-61 (Washington, D.C.: Oct. 6, 2004); *Financial Regulation: A Framework for Crafting and Assessing Proposals to Modernize the Outdated U.S. Financial Regulatory System*, GAO-09-216 (Washington, D.C.: Jan. 8, 2009); and *High-Risk Series: An Update*, GAO-09-271 (Washington, D.C.: January 2009).

[7] GAO-09-216. The framework included a total of nine characteristics: clearly defined regulatory goals; appropriately comprehensive; system-wide focus; flexibility and adaptability; efficiency and effectiveness; consistent consumer and investor protections; independence, prominence, authority, and accountability for regulators; consistent financial oversight; and minimal taxpayer exposure.

[8] GAO-09-271.

[9] Financial market utilities are multilateral organizations such as payment systems, central securities depositories, and central counterparties that provide the essential infrastructure to clear and settle payments and other financial transactions.

[10] Treasury, *Financial Research Fund FY 2013 President's Budget Submission* accessed Feb. 22, 2012, http://www.treasury.gov/about/budget-performance/Documents/14- FY 2013 FRF CJ. pdf.

[11] As will be discussed later in this report, the Dodd-Frank Act provided that FSOC may determine whether a nonbank financial company shall be supervised by the Federal Reserve and subject to prudential standards if it determines that material financial distress at the nonbank financial company, or the nature, scope, size, scale, concentration, interconnectedness, or mix of the activities of the company, could pose a threat to the financial stability of the United States. The act lists specific factors for FSOC to consider in making these determinations along with any other risk-related factors it deems appropriate.

Large bank holding companies (with total consolidated assets of $50 billion or more) are automatically subject to enhanced supervision and prudential standards, according to the act. The Secretary of the Treasury, with the approval of FSOC, establishes regulations for determining the assessments levied on these nonbank financial companies and large bank holding companies. The assessments are to take into account differences among the companies based on the considerations for establishing prudential standards and are to equal OFR's total expenses.

[12] The budget submission also included payments to FDIC for reimbursement of implementation expenses, such as rule writing and resolution planning, for about $5 million in fiscal year 2012 and about $11 million in fiscal year 2013.

[13] A substantial portion of OFR's basic services are performed through reimbursable arrangements with Treasury and through other interagency arrangements that fall under the contractual services category. Specifically, this includes reimbursable support from departmental offices within Treasury; benefits from OCC; and services from the Bureau of Public Debt including human resource, procurement, and financial management services.

[14] GAO, *Dodd-Frank Act Regulations: Implementation Could Benefit from Additional Analyses and Coordination*, GAO-12-151 (Washington, D.C.: Nov. 10, 2011).

[15] Basel II is a risk-based capital framework for banks based on an international accord. For more information on Basel II adoption in the United States, see GAO, *Risk-Based Capital: Bank Regulators Need to Improve Transparency and Overcome Impediments to Finalizing the Proposed Basel II Framework*, GAO-07-253 (Washington, D.C.: Feb. 15, 2007) and *Risk-Based Capital: New Basel II Rules Reduced Certain Competitive Concerns, but Bank Regulators Should Address Remaining Uncertainties*, GAO-08-953 (Washington, D.C.: Sept. 12, 2008).

[16] OFR's shorter-term activities will be discussed later in this report.

[17] GAO, *Millennium Challenge Corporation: Progress Made on Key Challenges in First Year of Operations,* GAO-05-625T (Washington, D.C.: Apr. 27, 2005) and *Troubled Asset Relief Program: Additional Actions Needed to Better Ensure Integrity, Accountability, and Transparency,* GAO-09-161 (Washington, D.C.: Dec. 2, 2008).

[18] See GAO, Internal Control: Standards for Internal Control in the Federal Government, GAO/AIMD-00-21.3.1 (Washington, D.C.: November 1999); and Internal Control Standards: Internal Control Management and Evaluation Tool, GAO-01-1008G (Washington, D.C.: August 2001). These standards reflect updates in private sector internal control guidance, including the issuance of *Internal Control—Integrated Framework* by the Committee of Sponsoring Organizations of the Treadway Commission (COSO). Also see COSO, *Enterprise Risk Management—Integrated Framework* (September 2004). For the importance of objectives and performance measures in determining accountability and efficiency, see, for example, GAO, *Results-Oriented Government: GPRA Has Established a Solid Foundation for Achieving Greater Results*, GAO-04-38 (Washington, D.C.: Mar. 10, 2004) and *Government Performance: GPRA Modernization Act Provides Opportunities to Help Address Fiscal, Performance, and Management Challenges,* GAO-11-466T (Washington, D.C.: Mar. 16, 2011).

[19] For a detailed description of all the committees, see appendix II.

[20] These authorities describe special jobs and situations for which it is impractical to use standard qualification requirements and to rate applicants using traditional competitive procedures. Under the Dodd-Frank Act, OFR must seek to maintain comparability of compensation and benefits with other Financial Institutions Reform, Recovery, and Enforcement Act agencies. Accordingly, OFR has adopted the pay and compensation system available at OCC to meet the requirement of the act.

[21] When OFR has a confirmed director, it will have some autonomy. For example, according to the Dodd-Frank Act, the director's congressional testimony is not to be subject to prior approval by any agency including Treasury or any other FSOC member.

[22] Council of Inspectors General on Financial Oversight, *Audit of the Financial Stability Oversight Council's Controls over Non-public Information* (Washington, D.C.: June 2012).

[23] See GAO, *Executive Guide: Effectively Implementing the Government Performance and Results Act*, GAO/GGD-96-118 (Washington, D.C.: June 1996) and *Results Oriented Cultures: Implementation Steps to Assist Mergers and Organizational Transformations*, GAO-03-669 (Washington, D.C.: July 2, 2003).

[24] Pub. L. No. 103-62, 107 Stat. 286 (1993), and as amended by the GPRA Modernization Act of 2010, Pub. L. No. 111-352, 124 Stat. 3866 (2011). Performance plans or budgets are intended to provide the direct linkage between an agency's longer-term goals (as defined in the strategic plan) and what its managers and staff are doing on a day-to-day basis and include how resources will be used to accomplish those goals. Performance updates provide feedback to managers, policymakers, and the public on what was actually accomplished for the resources expended.

[25] Agencies expending less than $20 million annually may request such an exemption. See 31 U.S.C. § 1117.

[26] OFR's budget submission will be included as part of the President's fiscal year 2014 budget submission that is expected to be released in February 2013.

[27] Department of the Treasury, Office of the Inspector General, *Dodd Frank Act: Treasury Has Made Progress to Stand-up the Office of Financial Research* (Washington, D.C.: June 27, 2012). The report noted that OFR took longer than expected to finalize a comprehensive implementation plan, which the OIG defined as including OFR's strategic framework, strategic roadmap, other planning documents and individual project plans. The report stated that progress going forward would depend on its ability to execute its plan and recommended that OFR's Chief Operating Officer monitor progress in carrying out the activities in the comprehensive implementation plan and take timely action to address any slippages or otherwise make adjustments to achieve the objectives and keep to the time frames in the plan.

[28] The Dodd-Frank Act requires individual members to submit a signed statement to Congress to accompany many FSOC reports saying whether they believe that FSOC, the government, and the private sector are taking all reasonable steps to ensure financial stability and mitigate systemic risk that would negatively affect the economy. If they did not believe this the statement would need to indicate what actions the member believes should be taken. 12 U.S.C. § 5322(b).

[29] FSOC officials noted that the procedures were marked draft because this is a new process and the committee expected to change the procedures based on its initial experience.

[30] In some circumstances, such as rapidly evolving risks, the discussion can be fast tracked to FSOC members for a discussion of potential responses.

[31] Dimitrios Bisias, Mark Flood, Andrew W. Lo, and Stavros Valavanis, *A Survey of Systemic Risk Analytics*, Office of Financial Research Working Paper #0001 (Washington, D.C.: Jan. 15, 2012).

[32] The Macroprudential Toolkit: Measurement and Analysis. Conference held in Washington, DC: December 1-2, 2011.

[33] Such a data-sharing exercise is akin to what the International Monetary Fund proposes with its Financial Soundness Indicators. See International Monetary Fund, *Financial Soundness Indicators: Compilation Guide* (Washington, D.C.: March 2006).

[34] Office of Financial Research, *2012 Annual Report* (Washington, D.C.: July 2012).

[35] The legal entity identifier is a new a universal standard for identifying all parties to financial contracts. This will be discussed in more detail later in the report.

[36] FSOC, Minutes of the Financial Stability Council: held October 11, 2011, accessed Jan. 17, 2012, http://www.treasury.gov/initiatives/fsoc/Pages/council-meeting-minutes.aspx.

[37] See, GAO *Troubled Asset Relief Program: Continued Stewardship Needed as Treasury Develops Strategies for Monitoring and Divesting Financial Interests in Chrysler and GM*, GAO-10-151 (Washington, D.C.: Nov. 2, 2009).

[38] 12 U.S.C. § 5322(a)(2)(E).

[39] 5 U.S.C. App. 2.

[40] The Dodd-Frank Act provides that member agencies, in consultation with OFR, must implement regulations promulgated by OFR to standardize the types and formats of data reported and collected on behalf of FSOC. However, it also explicitly notes that this provision does not supersede or interfere with the independent authority of a member agency under other law to collect data in such format as the agency requires.

[41] The President's Working Group on Financial Markets was established by an executive order in 1988, in response to the 1987 market crash. Executive Order 12631 of March 18, 1988, 15 U.S.C. § 78b note. The Federal Financial Institutions Examination Council (FFIEC) was established in 1979, pursuant to the Federal Financial Institutions Examination Council Act of 1978, 12 U.S.C. §§ 3301-3311. It is a formal interagency body empowered to prescribe uniform principles, standards, and report forms for the federal examination of financial institutions by the Federal Reserve, National Credit Union Administration, FDIC, OCC, and the State Liaison Committee, and to make recommendations to promote uniformity in the supervision of these financial institutions. The Dodd-Frank Act added the Consumer Financial Protection Bureau to FFIEC. The President's Working Group and FFIEC remain in place.

[42] The Group of 20 (G20) is a group of finance ministers and central bank governors from 19 countries—including the United States—and the EU. The Financial Stability Board brings together from the G20 countries central bank officials, finance and treasury officials, and financial institution regulators; officials of the International Monetary Fund and World Bank, and representatives from non-G20 countries to address issues related to global financial stability.

[43] See GAO-06-15. Other practices include developing mechanisms to monitor, evaluate, and report on results; reinforcing agency accountability for collaborative efforts through agency plans and reports; and reinforcing individual accountability for collaborative efforts through performance management systems.

[44] See GAO-12-151.

[45] See GAO-12-151.

[46] Section 102(a)(4) of the Dodd-Frank Act defines a nonbank financial company for purposes of title I of the act as a domestic or foreign company (other than a bank holding company or certain other types of firms) that is predominantly engaged in financial activities as specified in section 102(a)(6).

[47] The Dodd-Frank Act also subjects large bank holding companies with total consolidated assets of $50 billion or more to enhanced supervision and prudential standards. No FSOC designation is required for these bank holding companies to be subjected to enhanced supervision and standards. In addition, some potential nonbank holding companies that may be designated are already subject to some Federal Reserve oversight because they are thrift holding companies. The Dodd-Frank Act transferred the oversight of these companies from the Office of Thrift Supervision to the Federal Reserve.

[48] Other Dodd-Frank provisions impose additional requirements on large bank holding companies and nonbank financial companies designated by FSOC. These include a requirement that the Federal Reserve subject designated nonbank financial companies that engage in proprietary trading to additional capital requirements, the authority of CFTC to impose limitations on the ability of those companies to control derivative clearing organizations and exchanges, and the ability of FDIC to impose risk-based assessments on large bank holding companies and designated nonbank financial companies if necessary to repay any obligations issued by FDIC to Treasury under the orderly liquidation authority.

[49] 5 U.S.C. § 552.

[50] Pub. L. No. 111-203, § 112(d)(5), 124 Stat. 1397.

[51] A regulatory action is determined to be "economically significant" if the Office of Management and Budget determines that it is likely to have an annual effect on the economy of $100 million or more or adversely affect in a material way the economy, a

sector of the economy, productivity, competition, jobs, the environment, public health or safety, or state, local, or tribal governments or communities.

[52] Expert opinions differ on whether certain provisions in title II of the Dodd-Frank Act will lessen any cost advantage certain institutions have enjoyed.

[53] In GAO-12-151 we note the importance of setting up baselines early to support later retrospective reviews of individual rules. In addition, we reported that in light of its various statutory requirements, FSOC plans to assess the future impact of significant Dodd-Frank rules. Given these plans, we previously recommended that FSOC direct OFR to begin collecting the necessary data to carry out these analyses.

[54] The Dodd-Frank Act also mandated that the FSOC Chairperson report on the macroeconomic effects of risk retention requirements and the effects of the size and complexity of financial institutions on capital market efficiency and economic growth by January 2011. The National Credit Union Authority Clarification Act required FSOC to report on actions taken in response to a mandated study by GAO on the National Credit Union Administration's supervision of corporate credit unions and implementation of prompt corrective action. The report was issued in June 2012.

[55] The Executive Summary of FSOC's 2011 Annual Report acknowledges that there is a long run imbalance in the U.S. budget and that a solution to that imbalance is crucial to U.S. financial stability. However, the body of the report says that the current pricing of U.S. debt implies that markets assume that a solution to the long-term imbalance will be found, and the issue is not included as an emerging threat.

[56] FSOC's 2012 Annual Report notes that there are both short-term and longer-term risks associated with the U.S. fiscal situation saying that the situation represents a source of uncertainty for financial markets and the real economy. OFR's 2012 Annual Report identifies the U.S. fiscal situation as a concern noting that the risk of a sharp change in the demand for U.S. Treasury securities potentially threatens U.S. financial stability. Both reports continue to note that in the short run yields on U.S. debt are very low.

[57] Along with their FSOC support staff, we interviewed the Independent Member with Insurance Expertise, the State Insurance Commissioner, and the State Securities Commissioner. We also interviewed the Conference of State Banking Supervisors staff supporting the State Banking Supervisor member, but not the member himself. For those members who are heads of federal agencies, we generally held interviews with senior agency officials, but not with the FSOC principal member. We did not interview anyone at the Federal Insurance Office but did provide them with an opportunity to provide their views and arrange an interview, if needed.

[58] GAO, *Dodd-Frank Act Regulations: Implementation Could Benefit from Additional Analyses and Coordination*, GAO-12-151 (Washington, D.C.: Nov. 10, 2011).

In: Financial Stability Oversight Council ... ISBN: 978-1-62417-217-5
Editor: Nolan S. Compton

Chapter 2

FINANCIAL STABILITY OVERSIGHT COUNCIL CREATED UNDER THE DODD-FRANK WALL STREET REFORM AND CONSUMER PROTECTION ACT: FREQUENTLY ASKED QUESTIONS*

Financial Stability Oversight Council

Q: What is the Financial Stability Oversight Council and what will it do?

A: The Financial Stability Oversight Council (FSOC) has a clear statutory mandate that creates for the first time collective accountability for identifying risks and responding to emerging threats to financial stability. It is a collaborative body chaired by the Secretary of the Treasury that brings together the expertise of the federal financial regulators, an insurance expert appointed by the President, and state regulators.

The FSOC has important new authorities to constrain excessive risk in the financial system. For instance, the FSOC has authority to designate a nonbank financial firm for tough new supervision and therefore avoid the regulatory gaps that existed before the recent crisis. Closing these gaps in supervision

* This is an edited, reformatted and augmented version of a Financial Stability Oversight Council document released October 2010.

will help minimize the risk of a nonbank financial firm threatening the stability of the financial system.

Additionally, to help with the identification of emerging risks to financial stability, the FSOC can provide direction to, and request data and analyses from the newly created Office of Financial Research (OFR) housed within Treasury.

Q: How will the FSOC help maintain our nation's financial stability?

A: Prior to the crisis, the existing regulatory framework focused regulators narrowly on individual institutions and markets, which allowed supervisory gaps to grow and regulatory inconsistencies to emerge—in turn, allowing arbitrage and weakened standards. No single entity had responsibility for monitoring and addressing risks to financial stability, which too often involves different types of financial firms operating in and institutions across multiple markets and important parts of the system were left unregulated. The Dodd-Frank Wall Street Reform and Consumer Protection Act ("the Act") addresses these problems through the creation of the FSOC, which is authorized to:

- *Facilitate Regulatory Coordination*: The FSOC has a statutory duty to facilitate information sharing and coordination among the member agencies regarding domestic financial services policy development, rulemaking, examinations, reporting requirements, and enforcement actions. Through this role, the FSOC will help eliminate gaps and weaknesses within the regulatory structure, to promote a safer and more stable system.
- *Facilitate Information Sharing and Collection*: By statute, the FSOC has a duty to facilitate the sharing of data and information among the member agencies. In instances where the data available proves insufficient, the FSOC has the authority to direct the OFR to collect information from certain individual financial companies to assess risks to the financial system, including the extent to which a financial activity or financial market in which the financial company participates, or the financial company itself, poses a threat to the financial stability of the United States. The collection and analysis of this data will aid the FSOC and OFR in their shared goal of removing

blind spots in the financial system so that regulators will be more able to see the entire landscape and be better equipped to identify systemic risks and other emerging threats.

- *Designate Nonbank Financial Companies for Consolidated Supervision*: In the run up to the financial crisis, some of the firms which posed the greatest risk to the financial system were not subject to tough consolidated supervision. The Act gives the FSOC with the authority to require consolidated supervision of nonbank financial companies, regardless of their corporate form.
- *Designate Systemic Financial Market Utilities and Systemic Payment, Clearing, or Settlement Activities*: The Act authorizes the FSOC to designate financial market utilities and payment, clearing, or settlement activities as systemic, requiring them to meet prescribed risk management standards prescribed and heightened oversight by the Federal Reserve, the Securities and Exchange Commission, or the Commodities Futures Trading Commission.
- *Recommend Stricter Standards*: The FSOC has the authority to recommend stricter standards for the largest, most interconnected firms, including nonbanks, designated by the FSOC for Federal Reserve supervision. Moreover, where the FSOC determines that certain practices or activities pose a threat to financial stability, the FSOC may make recommendations to the primary financial regulatory agencies for new or heightened standards.
- *Break Up Firms that Pose a "Grave Threat" to Financial Stability*: The FSOC has a significant role in determining whether action should be taken to break up those firms that pose a "grave threat" to the financial stability of the United States.
- *Recommend Congress close specific gaps in regulation.*

Q: What can the American people expect from the FSOC?

A: Over the next year, the FSOC will work to establish processes for designating nonbank financial companies and financial market utilities, recommending stricter standards, for monitoring and reporting on systemic risk, and for monitoring the financial system for emerging risks. In the near term, the staffs of the FSOC member agencies are focused on fulfilling its statutory mandate, including four studies that are required to be completed by January 22, 2011. Illustrated by the items released in conjunction with the first meeting of the FSOC on October 1, 2010, work is already well underway. The

FSOC can help provide a coordination role among the member agencies to help bring agencies together and to coordinate complex interagency rulemakings, where appropriate. The FSOC released an integrated roadmap following its first meeting that is based on each independent agency's internal planning processes, which puts into the public domain timeframes statutory deadlines for key deliverables.

Q: Who does the FSOC report to?

A: The FSOC provides new accountability to Congress and the American people to address emerging threats to financial stability and to coordinate regulatory actions to address them. The FSOC will be held accountable through a requirement that the FSOC report to Congress annually and that the Chairperson testify on the FSOC's activities and emerging threats to financial stability. Moreover, the FSOC will report to Congress as appropriate on particular topics. For instance, the FSOC is required to conduct four studies in its first six months following enactment, including a report providing recommendations on implementation of the Volcker Rule.

Q: Will FSOC Meetings be open to the public?

A: The FSOC is committed to conducting its business in an open and transparent manner. The FSOC will open its meetings to the public whenever possible. At the same time, the central mission of the FSOC is to monitor systemic and emerging threats. This will require discussion of supervisory and other market-sensitive data, including information about individual firms, transactions and markets that may only be obtained if maintained on a confidential basis. Protection of this information will be necessary in order to prevent destabilizing market speculation that could occur if that information were to be disclosed.

Accordingly, the FSOC has adopted public transparency policies that enumerate the reasons that the Chairperson may close a meeting, in whole or in part. In any event, the FSOC commits to holding two open meetings each year. In addition, when FSOC Members are asked to vote on a draft of a proposed or final rule, the FSOC will make those agenda items open to the public.

Q: How has Treasury been working with other Federal agencies to form the FSOC?

A: The FSOC will operate under a committee structure to promote shared responsibility among the member agencies and to leverage the expertise that already exists at each agency. The FSOC will form committees around its various statutory responsibilities and core issues that relate closely to systemic risk where more than one agency has a significant interest.

The FSOC will require some independent staff to provide advice on statutory authorities and obligations, and to manage its document flow, records retention, and public records disclosure. A staff of policy experts, with many detailed by member agencies, will also be required to help coordinate the work of the committees and, where appropriate, complex inter-agency rule makings, to support FSOC functions such as designations, and to draft reports to Congress.

Q: Who serves on the FSOC?

A: The FSOC is made up of ten voting members – nine federal financial regulatory agencies and an independent member with insurance expertise – and five nonvoting members.

- *Voting Members*: The Secretary of the Treasury, who serves as the Chairperson of the FSOC, the Chairman of the Board of Governors of the Federal Reserve System, the Comptroller of the Currency, the Director of the Consumer Financial Protection Bureau, the Chairman of the Securities and Exchange Commission, the Chairperson of the Federal Deposit Insurance Corporation, the Chairperson of the Commodity Futures Trading Commission, the Director of the Federal Housing Finance Agency, the Chairman of the National Credit Union Administration Board, and an independent member with insurance expertise that is appointed by the President and confirmed by the Senate for a six-year term.
- *Nonvoting Members Who Serve in an Advisory Capacity*: The Director of the OFR, the Director of the Federal Insurance Office, a state insurance commissioner selected by the state insurance commissioners, a state banking supervisor chosen by the state banking supervisors, and a state securities commissioner designated by the

state securities supervisors. The state nonvoting members have two-year terms.

In: Financial Stability Oversight Council ... ISBN: 978-1-62417-217-5
Editor: Nolan S. Compton

Chapter 3

STRATEGIC FRAMEWORK: FY2012-FY2014*

Department of the Treasury

INTRODUCTION

In establishing the Office of Financial Research (OFR or Office), the framers of the Dodd-Frank Wall Street Reform and Consumer Protection Act, Public Law 111-203 (Dodd-Frank Act) recognized the need for better data and better analysis to help the Financial Stability Oversight Council (Council) and market participants assess and respond to threats to financial stability.

Of course, there will always be a fundamental uncertainty about the source of such threats. But better data and analysis can support the design of stronger financial shock absorbers and guardrails to reduce the risk of crises. They can also support earlier warning and effective responses to mitigate the effects of crises when they do occur and help draw lessons for the future.

This strategic framework takes as its foundation the statutory mandates from the Dodd-Frank Act. It outlines a mission, goals, objectives and implementation priorities that will help to ensure that the OFR's efforts and investments are well targeted. It reflects substantial consultations in the period since enactment of the Dodd-Frank Act with a full range of stakeholders, including Council members, their agencies and staff, members of Congress,

* This is an edited, reformatted and augmented version of an Office of Financial Research document released March 2012.

industry representatives, as well as academics, financial authorities, and other researchers.

An effective strategic framework involves adapting to changing circumstances, and the OFR must be nimble to achieve its mandate. The financial environment will continue to change rapidly, partly in response to an evolving regulatory architecture in the United States and around the globe. The OFR will confront uncertainties inherent to new organizations undergoing rapid growth and change. Thus, this first articulation of the OFR strategic framework covers a shorter horizon than would be expected for a mature organization and frequent reviews and validation will be appropriate. The OFR will adapt this framework as necessary and undertake a first review in no later than two years.

Purpose and Duties

As set forth in Section 153(a) of the Dodd-Frank Act, the OFR is to support the Council and member agencies by:

(1) collecting data on behalf of the Council, and providing such data to the Council and member agencies;
(2) standardizing the types and formats of data reported and collected;
(3) performing applied research and essential long-term research;
(4) developing tools for risk measurement and monitoring;
(5) performing other related services;
(6) making the results of the activities of the Office available to financial regulatory agencies; and
(7) assisting such member agencies in determining the types and formats of data authorized by this Act to be collected by such member agencies.

Establishing the OFR

The Dodd-Frank Act established the OFR within the Treasury Department as part of a broader financial reform effort to address weaknesses that the financial crisis laid bare.

The OFR's mission recognizes its mandate to provide the Financial Stability Oversight Council, its agencies, and the public with more and better data and analysis to help identify, monitor, and evaluate threats to financial stability.

MISSION

Serve the Council, its member agencies, and the public by improving the quality, transparency, and accessibility of financial data and information, by conducting and sponsoring research related to financial stability, and by promoting best practices in risk management.

GOALS AND OBJECTIVES

Consistent with the Dodd-Frank Act, the OFR has established five strategic goals that together would strengthen understanding by OFR stakeholders of a rapidly changing financial landscape:

1. Support the Council through the secure provision of high-quality financial data and analysis needed to monitor threats to financial stability
2. Develop and promote data-related standards and best practices
3. Establish a center of excellence for research on financial stability and promote best practices for financial risk management
4. Provide the public with key data and analysis, while protecting sensitive information
5. Establish the OFR as an efficient organization and world-class workplace

OFR STAKEHOLDERS

- *Council members, their agencies, and staff*
- The *Congress* and the *public*
- *Other financial authorities*, both foreign and domestic
- *Market participants*, both as providers of data and beneficiaries of the OFR's data and analysis
- *Research communities*, including academics and think tanks in the US and abroad

- *OFR staff* for opportunities to contribute and grow in an environment that supports excellence

Goal 1— Support the Council through the Secure Provision of High-Quality Financial Data and Analysis Needed to Monitor Threats to Financial Stability

Specific objectives under this goal are to:

- Provide research and analytical support to Council members, their agencies and staff to:
  - Monitor and interpret how financial market developments affect financial stability; and
  - Help them improve regulation of financial entities and markets.
- Serve as a secure Council-wide data utility.
  - Collect data n behalf of the Council and provide it to Council members, their agencies and staff where such data are essential to monitoring threats to financial stability and where they are not otherwise collected. Consistent with statute, this will include collecting, in coordination with the primary financial regulatory agency and in consultation with the Council, financial transaction and position data.
  - Provide Council members, their agencies and staff with timely access to financial data and metrics under rigorous data sharing and security protocols.
  - Reduce the reporting burden on financial institutions:
    - Coordinate data requests among Council member agencies with increasing reliance on standard identifiers and definitions, where possible; and
    - Sponsor shared data procurement and data management among Council member agencies to reduce duplication.
  - Enhance the quality and consistency of financial data available to Council member agencies:
    - Validate collected financial data; and

- Assist Council members, their agencies and staff through direct data services and technical support.
- Establish and maintain a catalog of the financial entities and instruments reported to the OFR.

Goal 2— Develop and Promote Data-Related Standards and Best Practices

Specific objectives under this goal are to:

- Facilitate, in collaboration with a broad range of stakeholders, the establishment of global data-related standards to improve data quality and scope, while also reducing costs of reporting for both financial market participants and Council member agencies.
- Assist Council member agencies in defining standards and best practices for data collection and management.

Goal 3— Establish a Center of Excellence for Research and Analysis on Financial Stability and Promote Best Practices in Risk Management

Specific objectives under this goal are to:

- Conduct and sponsor research to identify, monitor, and evaluate threats to financial stability, analyze disruptions as they occur, and to identify lessons learned thereafter.
- Evaluate and report on stress tests or other stability-related evaluations and provide advice on the impact of policies related to systemic risk.
- Promote best practices in financial risk management through evaluation of existing methods and governance, as well as development and promulgation of new methods.
- Establish forums for collaboration with outside stakeholders on these initiatives.

Goal 4— Provide the Public with Key Data and Analysis, While Protecting Sensitive Information

Specific objectives under this goal are to:

- Increase the transparency and distribution of research on the financial system, while safeguarding sensitive information, by publishing financial analysis, data and information. Publications will include:
  - Analytical reports, including an Annual Report to Congress and working paper series;
  - A financial company reference database;
  - A financial instrument reference database; and
  - Formats and standards for data required by the OFR.
- Testify on OFR activities and the OFR's assessment of significant financial market developments and potential emerging threats to financial stability.

Goal 5— Establish the Office of Financial Research as an Efficient Organization and World-Class Workplace

The key objectives under this goal are to:

- Build an effective workforce environment;
- Engage the workforce to achieve organizational success; and
- Support the OFR's mission in a cost-effective manner.

IMPLEMENTATION PRIORITIES

Building from progress to date and consistent with a core set of operating principles, the OFR is:

- Ramping up its services to Council members, their agencies and staff;
- Beginning to publish OFR data and analysis;
- Accelerating work to establish the secure information technology platforms and business systems critical to achieving its mission; and
- Continuing to reinforce its institutional infrastructure.

Progress to date and priorities for the coming period are detailed below, including the specific priorities for the Data Center and Research & Analysis Center.

OFR OPERATING PRINCIPLES

This core set of principles defines the characteristics the OFR strives to achieve:

- *Striving for excellence*: establish a reputation for world-class quality, objectivity, integrity, and impact related to research, data standards and data management practices;
- *Innovative*: expand boundaries of knowledge and technique to enhance understanding, identification, measurement, and management of threats to financial stability;
- *Transparent*: support and encourage publication of data, tools and research while ensuring sensitive data is strictly protected, and partner with regulatory, industry and academic experts, both domestically and internationally, to serve the needs of the Council and the public;
- *Efficient*: serve the needs of OFR stakeholders in a cost-effective manner and support efficiencies in data collection by only requesting data not already available; and
- *Multidisciplinary*: draw upon a full range of methodologies from the social sciences, technical disciplines, and industry practices to apply the best technique to a given task.

Data Center

The Dodd-Frank Act established the Data Center within the OFR to collect, validate, and maintain data from Council member agencies, publically available data sources, and financial entities. Working together with the Research & Analysis Center, the Data Center has begun to provide analytical and data-related services to the Council and its member agencies, for example, through support for the Council's Annual Report on financial stability, as well as data and analysis related to designation of nonbank financial companies for consolidated supervision by the Federal Reserve Board. The OFR has also supported the establishment of the Council Data Committee as a forum to discuss data-related issues among member agencies and is creating an inventory of Council data to support better coordination and reduced redundancies in data collection efforts.

A key early initiative of the OFR has been its work with policymakers, regulators, and the private sector on establishing a global Legal Entity Identifier (LEI) –work that contributed to the November 2011 G-20 Leaders endorsement in Cannes of a Group of Experts to establish the governance for an LEI. The initiative—driving toward one global standard to uniquely identify parties to financial transactions— will support better understanding of true exposures and interconnections among and across financial institutions and markets. This should improve the ability of both regulators and market participants to mitigate threats to the financial system.

An early priority for the Data Center has been to build the informational infrastructure needed to deliver on the OFR's data-related and analytical mandates. This requires the establishment of secure analytical and database platforms, implementation of sound business systems, and the steady expansion of data acquisition—through both shared procurement and efficient collection from financial institutions, consistent with the need to avoid duplicative and unnecessary requests. The OFR recognizes both the importance of rapid progress and the need to ensure that investments in information technology and business processes, infrastructure, and security structures are well-designed and cost-effective. To meet these twin needs, the OFR is establishing a secure short-term data and analytical IT environment to meet immediate needs, while initiating the design and planning of medium-term information and security architecture. As part of these efforts, the OFR is establishing robust controls and best-practice procedures, including strong data and information security protocols.

For the remainder of FY2012, the focus of OFR efforts is to:

- Develop and begin to implement a secure database and analytical computing environment.
    - Finalize work on a short-term, secure computing environment that will be leveraged for data storage and sharing and near-term analytical needs. This environment will also serve as the foundation for a robust analytical platform to serve longer-term needs.

- Complete pilot projects on data security and high-performance computing (utilizing appropriate best-practice expertise) to provide input into the OFR's medium-term data and analytical infrastructure, while also supporting near-term outputs.
- Taking these pilots on board, complete the initial design of a secure computing and data storage architecture and initiate implementation as soon as late 2012. Additional validation—including from information technology and data experts, as well as from data end-users— will be critical both prior to implementation and at multiple stages of the implementation process.
- Establish access, initially for Council members, their agencies and staff, to a preliminary set of selected financial data and metrics.
- As a first step in supporting data coordination among Council member agencies, inventory financial data held by these stakeholders.
- Continue to acquire the data necessary to support the Council's designations process and other needs of Council members, their agencies and staff, and initiate secure data provision for the OFR Research & Analysis Center.
- Continue to support the Data Committee of the Council as a forum for collaboration on data-related issues, including assistance on prioritizing OFR data initiatives and establishment of data sharing protocols.

- Promote and strengthen standards for financial data.
    - Continue to play an active role in building consensus for and facilitating adoption of a global LEI, including through the support of a Financial Stability Board experts group established in December 2011 to move the LEI forward and continued work with U.S. financial regulators—such as the Securities and Exchange Commission and Commodity Futures Trading Commission—on incorporation of the LEI into their rulemaking.
    - Work with public and private partners, both domestically and internationally, to identify and prioritize gaps in financial data standards beyond LEI where standardization would improve data quality, the ability to aggregate, risk management standards, and the exchange of data among Council members.

Research & Analysis Center

The Research & Analysis Center was established within the OFR by the Dodd-Frank Act to develop and maintain independent analytical capabilities and computing resources to monitor, investigate, and report on risks to financial stability. As noted above, the OFR has begun to provide analytical support to the Council and it member agencies. In addition, it launched a Research Seminar Series last fall and a Working Paper Series in January, with its first Annual Report to Congress to be provided this summer. The OFR has also begun to build a virtual community of researchers, academics, and practitioners that can collaborate on its research.

Achieving the OFR's mission will ultimately require new methods for measuring, analyzing, and representing conditions in the financial system, with special emphasis on leverage, maturity, liquidity, credit transformation, and linkages within and between the financial system and economic activity. Advancing research in the areas highlighted below will be an iterative process as the OFR's analytical infrastructure is developed, data are collected, and requirements are refined, with activities focused on:

- For the benefit of the Council and broader stakeholders, proactive monitoring and reporting on the system-wide risk levels and patterns, through, for example, recurring narrative reports that explain the state of and threats to the financial system (including the report), and related studies examining particular risks to financial stability, risk management methods and tools, and relationships between financial and other economic activities;
- Contributions to rapid response analytics on significant financial events;
- Forensic analyses of significant events affecting financial stability;
- Evaluations of stability-related assessments and advice on the impact of policies aimed at promoting financial stability, looking across the entire financial system. Examples might include stress-testing and related capital and liquidity planning exercises, tools that influence funding and market liquidity and the connections between them, and tools to limit leverage and maturity mismatches;
- Promotion of best practices in risk management through the development and promulgation of methods to measure risks, including liquidity risk, counterparty risk, market risk and credit risk; the evaluation of methods in current use, considering their effectiveness

at the individual firm and systemic level and their potential effects on the broader financial system; and collaboration with regulators, industry participants, and academics to highlight and advance good governance of the risk management function in financial firms;
- Conferences, colloquia, and seminars on issues related to financial stability and risk management; and
- An online resource for researchers, including OFR Working Papers and tools for risk analytics.

During FY2012, key priorities include work to:

- Develop the capacity to conduct, coordinate, and sponsor initial research including by:
  - Collaborating with the Council to develop and maintain a "dashboard" of metrics and indicators related to financial stability initially drawn from previous academic research and supported by the Data Center;
  - Responding to research requests on regulatory impact from member agencies; and
  - Conducting broader studies and providing advice on the impact of policies related to treats to financial stability (e.g., on funding markets and interconnections across the financial system).
- Develop and disseminate analyses of risk management tools that may include such topics as stress testing, contingent capital, robust risk measurement, methods for quantifying counter-party risk in derivatives markets, and models of risk propagation through financial linkages.
- With the OFR Data Center, launch vehicles for collaboration and publication of data and analysis on financial stability:
  - Publish the OFR's first Annual Report on or before July 2012;
  - Publish additional research and data on issues related to threats to financial stability, including through the OFR Working Paper Series;
  - Building from the December 2011 OFR-Council Conference, "The Macroprudential Toolkit: Measurement and Analysis," support public-private dialogue on issues relevant to the OFR's mandate; and
  - Expand the Research Seminar Series.

Building the OFR

The OFR has made substantial progress in building the initial institutional functions to support its core missions. A key upfront objective was to define the scope of the OFR's mission, starting from the foundation established in the legislation and building through outreach and broad-based consultations. Establishing an initial organizational and workforce plan, as well as operational processes and controls, have also been priorities. Foundational work on the OFR's human resources strategy was articulated in the OFR's first report to Congress on these issues in September 2011. The OFR has made substantial progress in filling key management positions, made early inroads in broader staffing, and begun to build working relationships with outside thought leaders. In September, the Department of the Treasury, with the concurrence of the Office of Government Ethics, issued an interim rule establishing post-employment restrictions for OFR employees with access to sensitive data, as required by the Dodd-Frank Act. Work on the OFR's Washington facility is also well advanced.

The OFR is continuing to build the organizational structures, processes, and controls needed to support strategic decision-making, ensure efficient use of resources, and support transparent performance measurement and responsiveness to external review. Priorities for FY2012 include:

- Attract and retain the highly trained, experienced staff needed to fulfill the OFR's mission.
    - Further elaborate OFR human resource plans for recruitment and retention (including through an OFR Fellowship Program), training and workforce development, and workforce flexibility. Report on progress to Congress, consistent with requirements under the Dodd-Frank Act.
    - Continue active recruitment to build expertise across the range of needed competencies.
- Create an advisory committee of leading researchers, academics, data managers and IT experts to help the OFR identify issues, evaluate work product, and recruit talent.
- Establish a sound strategic and operational framework.
    - Expand initial policies and procedures to support sound and efficient operations and rigorous internal controls.

- Link programmatic, human resources, and budgetary decision-making to the strategic framework, including through an OFR program management function.
- Develop performance measurement and risk management systems appropriate to a maturing organization.

- Continue to address OFR facilities requirements.
- Ensure that the OFR operates on a sound financial footing.
    - Assist in preparations for a Treasury rule to establish a permanent financing source for the OFR through assessments on certain financial institutions.

Table 1. Summary of Goals, Objectives, and FY2012 Implementation Priorities

Goals	Objectives	FY2012 Implementation Priorities

Council Support	• Analytic Support
	• Council-wide Data Utility
	  • Collect necessary data
	  • Promote efficiency and security in data acquisition
	  • Enhance data quality and consistency
	  • Catalog financial entities and instruments
		• Respond to Council research requests focusing initially on designation issues
		• Develop and begin to implement a secure analytical environment
		• Establish timely access to initial financial data and metrics
		  • Deliver initial Council-wide data inventory
		  • Maintain "dashboard" of metrics/flexible graphics
		  • Undertake initial data acquisition
		  • Support Council Data Committee

Promotion of Data-Related Standards	• Facilitate establishment of data-related standards • Assist Council in defining standards and best practices for data collection	• Facilitate adoption of a global LEI • Identify additional standards to enhance data processing efficiencies
Center for Research	• Conduct and sponsor research on financial stability • Promote best practices in risk management • Facilitate coordination and joint research	• Conduct studies on impact of policies related to financial stability • Develop and disseminate analyses of risk management tools • OFR-Council Conference: *The Macroprudential Toolkit: Measurement and Analysis* • Research Seminar Series

Table 1. (Continued)

Goals	Objectives	FY2012 Implementation Priorities
Public Information	• Publication of analytical reports, data and related information including reference databases and formats/standards for data • Annual Testimony	• OFR Annual Report • OFR Working Paper Series
Building the OFR	• Effective management of human and financial capital	• Elaborate strategies to attract and retain talent, including through OFR Fellowship Program • Create Advisory Committee of leading researchers academics, data managers and IT experts • Continue to build a sound strategic and operational framework • Address OFR facility requirements • Assist in rulemaking to establish permanent financial source

APPENDIX ONE. OFR ORGANIZATION AND WORKFORCE PLAN

Roles and Responsibilities

The OFR's Organizational structure takes as its starting point the requirements set out in the Dodd-Frank Act, including with respect to the role of the Director and the mission of the Data Center and Research & Analysis Center. The organization also recognizes the importance of a "one-organization" approach—with close coordination in the work of the Data and Research & Analysis Centers.

Director

The OFR Director, appointed by the President, with the advice and consent of the Senate, provides overall leadership, direction, and representation for the OFR. The Director also serves as a non-voting member of the Council. Key duties, as stipulated under the Dodd-Frank Act, include:

- In consultation with the Chairperson of the Council, establishing the as well as the size of and compensation for OFR staff.

- Reporting to and testifying before the Committee on Banking, Housing, and Urban Affairs of the Senate and the Committee on Financial Services of the House of Representatives annually on the activities of the Office, including the work of the Data Center and the Research and Analysis Center, and the assessment by the Office of significant financial market developments and potential emerging threats to the financial stability of the United States. The OFR Director's testimony is not subject to prior review by any office or agency and shall state that the views expressed are those of the Director.
- Requiring from a financial company, by subpoena, the production of data not elsewhere available, where necessary to carry out the functions of the OFR, after coordinating with the relevant primary financial regulatory agency.
- Ensuring that data collected and maintained by the Data Center are kept secure and protected against unauthorized disclosure.
- Ensuring that all other requirements for the OFR under the Dodd-Frank Act are fulfilled.

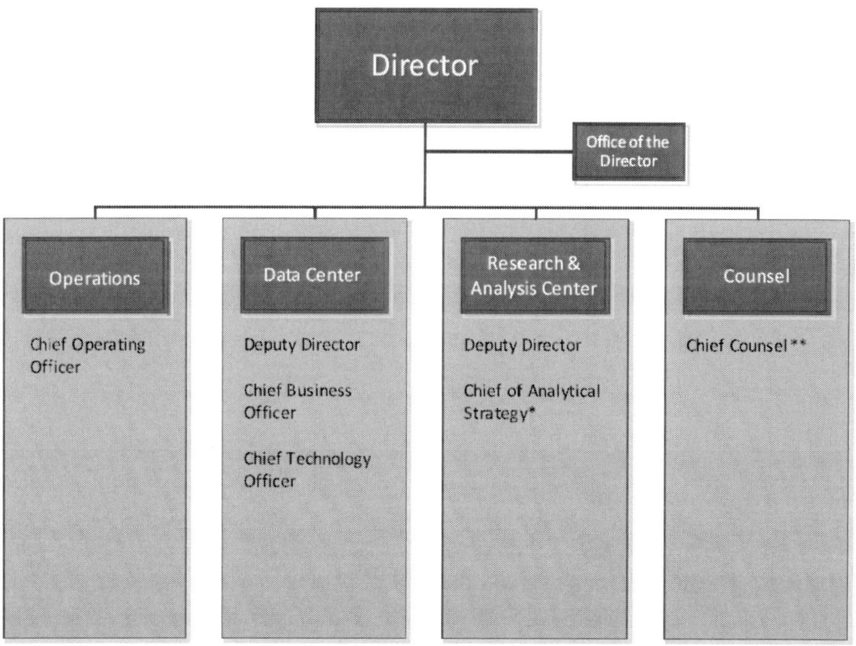

* Reports_ to_ OFR_ Director

** Reports_ to_ Treasury_ General_ Counsel

Data Center

Deputy Director, Data Center

The Deputy Director of the Data Center reports to and advises the Director of the OFR, liaises with stakeholders, and directs the full range of operations of the OFR's Data Center, covering business operations, information technology, as well as OFR-wide program management. In this context, the Deputy Director provides strategic guidance to prioritization of activities and investments required to fulfill the OFR's mission as it relates to secure data collection and management, data standards, and data services to the Council and broader stakeholders.

Chief Business Officer

The Chief Business Officer (CBO) reports to and advises the Deputy Director of the Data Center, liaises with stakeholders, and manages the Data Center business groups on data management and analytical operations. In this context, the CBO coordinate s closely with the Deputy Director of Research & Analysis, the Chief Technology Officer and the Chief Operating Officer.

The CBO directs data identification, acquisition, management and distribution to the Council and broader stakeholders, as appropriate. The CBO assists in the identification and development of data-related standards required to analyze threats to financial stability.

Chief Technology Officer

Reporting to the Deputy Director of the Data Center, the Chief Technology Officer (CTO) provides leadership and advice to senior management of the OFR on the use and management of information technology to support achievement of the OFR's mission. This function directs and manages the technical build of the Data Center and the maintenance of information security policies and control mechanisms.

The CTO function includes the governance and management of IT services through a sound, secure, and integrated information technology architecture and roadmap for the OFR. The roadmap ensures that systems architecture, standards and protocols provide an efficient, innovative, and secure environment to house and disseminate the OFR's information assets as appropriate to support the OFR mission.

Research & Analysis Center

Deputy Director, Research & Analysis

The Deputy Director of Research & Analysis reports to and advises the Director of the OFR, liaises with stakeholders, and directs the full range of operations of the OFR's Research and Analysis Center.

The Deputy Director of Research & Analysis sets out the strategic priorities and overall direction for the Research and Analysis Center, in close consultation with the Director. The Deputy Director is also responsible for oversight of research staff and of programs for collaboration with the outside research community.

Chief of Analytical Strategy

The Chief of Analytical Strategy (CAS) reports to and advises the Director of the OFR and supports a broad range of analytical and operational functions related to the OFR's research function, in coordination with the Deputy Director of Research & Analysis and the Deputy Director of the Data Center.

The CAS directs the design, development and delivery of comprehensive, integrated analytical strategies and implementation plans on critical issues having broad impact on research programs and activities. The CAS also supports, in close collaboration with the Deputy Director of Research & Analysis, the management of the OFR's research functions, including definition of strategic analytical priorities and resulting data acquisition requirements, as well as plans for recruitment, outreach and collaboration with outside experts.

Support Offices

Chief Operating Officer

The Chief Operating Officer (COO), reporting to and advising the Director of the OFR, is responsible for overall allocation, management, and oversight of resources to achieve the OFR's mission and, in collaboration with OFR senior management, for the establishment of programs supporting the stand-up of the OFR.

The COO oversees OFR-wide communications, strategic planning and performance measurement and has broad responsibilities for establishing and overseeing implementation of the OFR's governance framework, including internal OFR operational policies, procedures, and controls. The COO oversees, in collaboration with the Treasury Department's Assistant Secretary for Management, the human resources, procurement, facilities, and financial management of the OFR.

Chief Counsel

The Chief Counsel serves as chief legal advisor to the Director of the OFR and directs all legal activities of the OFR, reporting to Treasury's Office of the General Counsel. In this capacity, the Chief Counsel coordinates legal issues with the legal counsel for the Council as related to the OFR's work and data collection performed for the Council.

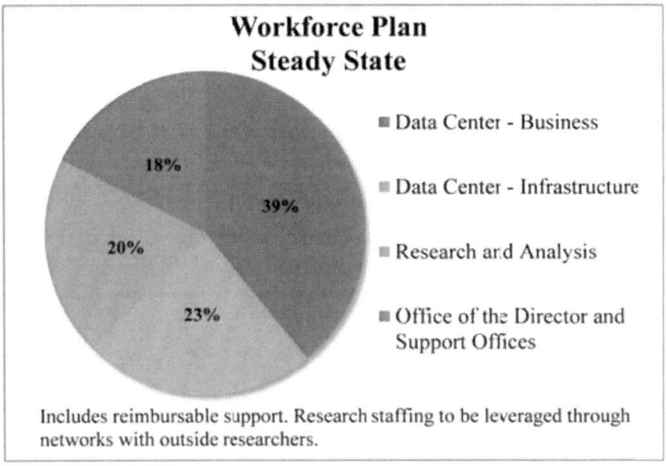

Workforce Plan

The OFR has put in place an initial workforce plan to build the capabilities needed to achieve its mission. The plan recognizes the broad range of core competencies required by the office, including data management and analytics, data standardization and best practices, information technology, macroeconomics, financial market and institution analysis, statistics and risk management, and applied sciences, as well as program management, legal services, communications, strategy, and resource management. The Dodd-Frank Act emphasized use f efficient and innovative structures to attract and retain needed talent, including fellowships and partnerships with outside experts. The OFR has put in place an ambitious but achievable plan to build to steady state staffing levels (approximately 275-300 staff) within the next twenty-four to thirty-six months.

Appendix Two. Governance, Transparency, and Oversight

The OFR was established within the Department of the Treasury, Departmental Offices. In this context, Treasury's Assistant Secretary for Management supports the OFR through operational controls and procedures related to, *inter alia*, financial management, procurement, and human resources.

The OFR consults closely with the Treasury Secretary, including in his role as Council Chairperson, and other senior Treasury officials on strategic issues related to the OFR stand-up, including through participation in regular meetings on the Dodd-Frank Act's implementation chaired by the Deputy Secretary of the Treasury. The OFR also consults closely with the Council, as detailed below.

Financial Management and Human Resources

The OFR budget is set by the Director, in consultation with the Chairperson of the Council. OFR financial management follows Treasury protocols, and the financial activities and controls are reviewed as part of the broader audit of Departmental Offices within the Treasury. Information on the OFR budget is published as part of the President's Budget. The OFR is also assisted in the preparation of a Treasury rule to establish a permanent financing source for the OFR through assessments on certain financial institutions.

Internal OFR budget formulation, execution and control procedures, including regular reporting and review, have been established and are being further refined to reinforce sound fiscal management and to control costs. Specific policies and procedures relevant to resource allocation (e.g., training) are being further elaborated, building from existing Treasury guidance, where appropriate.

THE OFR AND THE COUNCIL

The primary function of the OFR is to support the FSOC and its member agencies in fulfilling their duty to promote financial stability and enhance market discipline. To do so, the Director of the OFR will work closely with the Chairperson of the FSOC (the Secretary of the Treasury).

The OFR serves as a data and research resource for the FSOC and its member agencies and works with those agencies to reduce reporting burdens and increase market transparency. In this context, the OFR serves as a shared resource for Council members, their agencies and staff. It is unique among those agencies because its primary mission is to analyze threats to the stability of the overall financial system, and because it has the authority to collect information, where needed, from any U.S. financial company. The OFR has a responsibility to evaluate and report on stress tests and other stability-related assessments of financial entities overseen by member agencies, provide advice to member agencies on the impact of their policies as they relate to financial stability, investigate disruptions and failures in the financial markets, and provide its analysis to the Council, Congress, and the public.

The OFR works closely with Council staff, who support policy discussions among and recommendations by the Council, e.g., at Council Committee meetings, through Council work streams, and in the Council's annual report. The OFR provides data and analysis to support that work, either as a participant or in response to requests from Council members, their agencies and staff. The OFR will have the capacity to provide in-depth, long-term research as well as rapid analyses of significant financial events to inform the policy debate that Council staff will coordinate.

Initial human resources policies have been established for the OFR, building from existing Treasury guidance, as amended to reflect statutory requirements for the OFR. Treasury-based controls for OFR hiring are being executed to support sound implementation, and tracking systems for hiring and staffing (based on the OFR's workforce plan) have been established and are being further refined to support internal OFR monitoring.

Program Management

The OFR is committed to establishing and maintaining strict and transparent processes for ensuring its resources are effectively assigned and its activities are well directed to support achievement of its strategic goals and requirements under the Dodd-Frank Act. An initial framework for project-related decision making, tracking and review has been established, which will help to maintain strong links between OFR investments and activities and its strategic goals and Dodd-Frank Act requirements.

The OFR Program Management Office (PMO) administers the project management function. To facilitate project tracking through all stages of implementation, the PMO is building and maintaining a comprehensive inventory of programs, projects, and activities.

During FY2012, the OFR will also create initial operational metrics to measure the organization's performance.

Information Security

Effective execution of the OFR's mission depends on the development and implementation of best-practice information and data management systems, including strong security controls and well-defined data distribution protocols. Establishment of robust access control systems and policies, as well as data-sharing protocols with Council members and other OFR stakeholders, are priorities for FY2012.

Transparency & External Evaluations

The OFR recognizes the need for transparency in its operations and financing. As noted, information on the OFR budget is published as part of the President's budget, and information regarding the OFR's strategic framework and performance monitoring will also be published. Publications related to the OFR's core operations, including the OFR Annual Report and required reports to Congress on OFR human resources, will provide additional visibility into the OFR's operations.

The OFR is also subject to external oversight and receives external input on its programs and procedures through three distinct channels:

- *Office of the Inspector General (OIG)*: The OIG conducts reviews of OFR operations, providing valuable input into the OFR strategic management process. A first engagement was initiated in June 2011.
- *Government Accountability Office (GAO)*: The GAO will conduct periodic reviews of the OFR. A first review covering the stand-up was initiated in November 2011.
- *Annual Testimony*: Under the Dodd-Frank Act, the OFR Director testifies before Congress annually on the activities of the Office.

In: Financial Stability Oversight Council ... ISBN: 978-1-62417-217-5
Editor: Nolan S. Compton

Chapter 4

DODD-FRANK ACT: TREASURY HAS MADE PROGRESS TO STAND-UP THE OFFICE OF FINANCIAL RESEARCH*

Department of the Treasury

ABBREVIATIONS

CFPB	Consumer Financial Protection Bureau
DO	Departmental Offices, Department of the Treasury
FRB	Board of Governors of the Federal Reserve System
FSOC	Financial Stability Oversight Council
GPRA	Government Performance and Results Act
IT	Information Technology
LEI	Legal Entity Identifier
OFR	Office of Financial Research

* This is an edited, reformatted and augmented version of an Audit Report (OIG-12-057) by the Department of the Treasury, Office of Inspector General, released June 27, 2012.

June 27, 2012

Michele Shannon
Chief Operating Officer

The Dodd-Frank Wall Street Reform and Consumer Protection Act (Dodd-Frank), enacted July 21, 2010, created the Office of Financial Research (OFR) within the Department of the Treasury to support the Financial Stability Oversight Council (FSOC) and its member agencies.[1] This report presents the results of our audit of Treasury's activities to establish OFR as of April 2012. This audit was included in the *Office of Inspector General Fiscal Year 2011 Annual Plan*.

Our audit objective was to evaluate the effectiveness and status of Treasury's process to establish OFR in a manner that achieves its legislative mandate. We conducted our field work from June 2011 through April 2012. We interviewed OFR and Treasury management personnel responsible for establishing OFR and reviewed documentation provided by OFR. Appendix 1 contains a more detailed description of our objective, scope, and methodology.

In brief, we found that, in the 21 months since OFR was created, efforts to establish the office are still in progress. The officials responsible for establishing OFR initially engaged in high-level strategic and organizational planning and sought to hire key personnel. They also focused their attention on developing and facilitating the global acceptance of a universal Legal Entity Identifier (LEI),[2] while leveraging Treasury's Departmental Offices (DO) to support OFR's administrative functions. In Summer 2011, after key operational personnel were brought on board, progress toward establishing a comprehensive implementation planning and project management process accelerated. This culminated in the approval of OFR's Project Management Methodology in January 2012, OFR's Strategic Framework in March 2012, and OFR's Strategic Roadmap in April 2012. While not finalized until well over a year after it was established, these documents and methodology, taken together, now provide OFR with a comprehensive implementation plan. This plan lays out the expected evolution of OFR's capabilities, reaching a mature state by fiscal year 2016. Concurrent with the development of its comprehensive implementation plan, OFR also began to develop its analytic and data support for FSOC, and its Research and Analysis Center has sponsored seminars and published two working papers on risk assessment topics.

We are recommending that OFR monitor its progress in carrying out the activities in the comprehensive implementation plan and take actions timely to address any slippages or otherwise make adjustments so as to achieve the objectives and timeframes in the plan.

In a written response, OFR provided its planned corrective action which we consider responsive to our recommendation.

Background

Title I of Dodd-Frank created OFR to support FSOC and its members. The act details the types of support to be provided including data collection, research, and risk measurement and monitoring. OFR is expected to improve the quality of financial data available to policymakers and facilitate a more robust and sophisticated analysis of the financial system. OFR is to be headed by a Presidentially appointed, Senate-confirmed Director. On December 16, 2011, the President nominated Mr. Richard Berner to serve as OFR Director. Although the Director position currently remains vacant while Mr. Berner's confirmation is under consideration in the U.S. Senate, Mr. Berner is assisting in the stand-up of the OFR in his capacity as Counselor to the Secretary of the Treasury.

To execute its mission functions, OFR is in the process of standing up two primary operational centers: (1) a data center to acquire, validate, maintain, and distribute the data necessary to help regulators identify vulnerabilities in the financial system as a whole, and to develop and promote data standards; and (2) a research and analysis center to conduct, coordinate, and sponsor research to support and improve regulation of financial firms and markets. Dodd-Frank gives the OFR Director significant latitude in determining the methods used to achieve its legislative mandate. While Dodd-Frank does not set a deadline for the office to be fully stood up, it does set a deadline of July 21, 2012, for OFR's first required congressional reporting on the state of the U.S. financial system.

Dodd-Frank also requires the Board of Governors of the Federal Reserve System (FRB) to fund OFR's operations for an initial period of 2 years, through July 21, 2012.[3] After the initial funding period, OFR is to be funded by an assessment on large bank holding companies and non-bank financial companies.[4] Treasury issued a final rule establishing this assessment for bank holding companies and an interim final rule establishing the assessment for non-bank financial companies on May 21, 2012, with the first assessments to occur on July 20, 2012[5].

Results of Review

Progress toward Stand-Up Made, and Comprehensive Planning and Implementation Efforts are Underway

Based on our review of planning documents and interviews with officials, we found that OFR developed initial high-level plans to identify the resources and infrastructure needed to achieve its legislative mandate. In the beginning, Treasury officials responsible for standing-up OFR were focusing on two areas:

- Promoting and obtaining global acceptance of an LEI system which is expected to provide the mechanism that will make it possible for regulators and market participants to understand more fully the interconnections and exposures among and across financial institutions and markets and thereby improve their ability to identify and mitigate threats to the financial system; and,
- Leveraging DO administrative support; specifically, human resources, information systems, procurement, budget and accounting processes, while supplementing them as needed with OFR-specific policies and procedures.

Progress has been made toward broader acceptance of an LEI and in standing up the administrative functions needed to support OFR. In addition, OFR has begun providing analytic and data support for FSOC and has produced a number of products through its Research and Analysis Center. However, OFR has just recently, in April 2012, finalized the longer-term component of its comprehensive implementation plan that lays out how it will stand up all of its activities and functions. The status of each OFR key operational component, as of the end of our field work, is discussed in the remainder of this report.

Organizational Structure and Human Resources

OFR has laid out an organizational structure that accounts for its mandated functional units and addresses its administrative needs. DO is currently providing OFR with human resources capabilities to support its staffing efforts. OFR is using existing DO practices where possible, but has also established OFR-specific human resource policies, where needed, including a uniform pay and classification system. According to officials, OFR projects that it will have 212 employees on-board by the end of fiscal year 2012. As of May 7, 2012, OFR had 78 employees on-board and filled 5 of its 8 executive positions. As of that date, one of the executives, the Chief Business Officer, was serving as the Acting Deputy Director of the Data Center.

As noted previously, a nominee for the position of OFR Director has been announced. In the absence of a Director, OFR can perform its operational functions under the Treasury Secretary's authority.

Data Standards, Research, and Analysis

OFR is working with the FSOC and its member agencies, directly and through the FSOC Data Committee, to evaluate data requirements of the FSOC and work to deliver needed data and metrics. To this end, OFR is currently engaged in a long term project to inventory data that is purchased, collected, or derived by FSOC member agencies. According to OFR's project tracking reports, the purchased data inventory has been completed, the collected data inventory is to be completed by August 2012, and the derived data inventory is to be completed by September 2013. OFR has prepared reports for FSOC consisting of metrics and indicators related to financial stability drawn from previous academic research.

OFR's Research and Analysis Center has established forums and networks to allow experts within and outside the regulatory system to contribute to OFR's mission. For example, on December 1 and 2, 2011, OFR hosted a conference entitled *The Macroprudential Toolkit: Measurement and Analysis* where regulators, academics, and industry representatives discussed issues related to systemic risk monitoring. OFR also collaborated with outside researchers to produce working papers on risk assessment topics and engaged the academic community in a series of OFR-sponsored research seminars.

OFR officials believe establishing a globally accepted LEI system is of great importance. Specifically, they expect that the acceptance of such a system will provide the mechanism that will make it possible for regulators and market participants to understand more fully the interconnections and exposures among and across financial institutions and markets and thereby improve their ability to identify and mitigate threats to the financial system. In November 2010, OFR published a statement of policy with a request for comment which defined the characteristics of a functional LEI system and OFR's intention to require the use of such a system in data reported to it.[6]

While it was originally anticipated that such a system would be established and adopted by mid-2011, expectations have been revised in light of challenges in gaining global support and acceptance for a universal LEI. OFR now expects global acceptance by mid-2012, with a phased rollout by transaction class and geographic region over a 2- to 5-year period.

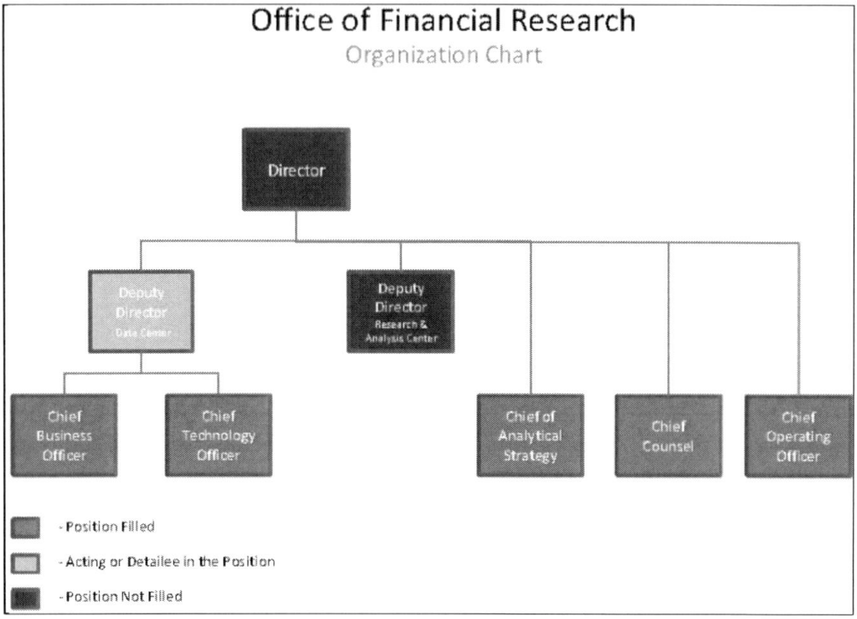

Source: OFR

Figure. OFR Organization Chart.

Information Technology and Operational Processes

OFR is scoping out its information technology (IT) and IT security infrastructure, operational and organizational governance processes, and stakeholder coordination and communication methods. These things are all necessary for OFR to meet its legislative mandate. OFR's current plan calls for a sequential strategy, beginning this fiscal year, where the foundations for OFR's capabilities with regard to data collection, analysis, research, and collaboration with FSOC member agencies are to be established. This is to be followed by a continued development of IT and business systems with the goal of satisfying immediate needs while reaching a mature state by fiscal year 2016.

OFR is leveraging DO's local area network and IT infrastructure, including office productivity systems and other software to perform work. At the time of our review, OFR had augmented these resources to establish a short term analytical environment. OFR officials told us that this analytical environment is maintained within a segregated portion of the DO network which has been secured in accordance with OFR-specific needs. The officials also told us that all systems used are maintained in accordance with DO security policies and procedures and that access to sensitive data is restricted to only those individuals whose job responsibilities require it.

Administrative Functions

OFR entered into a reimbursable services agreement with the Treasury Franchise Fund's Administrative Resource Center at the Bureau of the Public Debt to provide its payroll, budgeting, finance and accounting, and procurement services. OFR officials told us that critical internal control procedures have been implemented. Written policies and procedures have been developed for the budget execution and acquisition process. DO policies and procedures are currently being used for other processes such as budget formulation and financial reporting. OFR is currently evaluating whether further OFR-specific procedures are required.

Budget and Performance

OFR's fiscal year 2011 estimated budget was $34 million. During the year, OFR made funding requests of $13.1 million from FRB, of which $11.3 million was spent or obligated as of September 30, 2011. OFR's fiscal year 2012 estimated budget is $109.7 million, of which $20.4 million was obligated or outlayed as of March 31, 2012. The fiscal year 2013 budget request shows OFR's estimated expenses at $138.2 million.

OFR officials told us that they have not yet developed performance measures for the office. However, they plan to establish performance measures during fiscal year 2012 and to implement them beginning in fiscal year 2013. The importance of performance measures for gauging the progress and influencing the management of programs and projects at all levels of an agency is well recognized. Requirements and guidelines for such measures are in the Government Performance and Results Act of 1993 (GPRA) as amended by the GPRA Modernization Act of 2010.[7] Until performance measures are developed and implemented, OFR may be at a disadvantage in effectively communicating/demonstrating its accomplishments.

Assessments

As noted above, on January 3, 2012, Treasury exposed a rule for public comment that would establish OFR's assessment methodology. Treasury issued a final rule establishing this assessment for bank holding companies and an interim final rule establishing the assessment for non-bank financial companies on May 21, 2012, with the first assessments to occur on July 20, 2012.

Comprehensive Implementation Plan

The development of a comprehensive implementation plan as early as possible in standing up a new organization and the regular measurement of progress against that plan are recognized best practices. OFR's planning activities have evolved over time. For over a year after it was established, OFR pursued high-level planning activities, but did not develop a comprehensive implementation plan or employ formal project tracking capability to help lay it out, control, and monitor the development and deployment of its infrastructure and operational processes.

The operations and project managers needed to develop a formal, detailed and comprehensive implementation plan, along with project tracking capability to monitor the progress, were not brought on board until the summer of 2011. Since then, notable progress has been made. A Program Management Office was established in August 2011 and it began to implement a project management methodology. That methodology was finalized and approved in January 2012.

OFR's Program Management Office provides documentation of key decisions regarding the design and execution of critical deliverables, infrastructure, processes, policies, and procedures. The methodology it is using also provides for documented approval of decisions by the appropriate level of management or governing committee. Among other things, the methodology requires that OFR define required workstreams, assign accountability for completion, and set the milestones and due dates against which progress is measured and reported. Beginning in late 2011, OFR developed project plans with workstreams, milestones, and project due dates for certain critical near-term projects, such as preparing the first mandated OFR annual report.[8]

OFR also developed a strategic plan which was approved by Treasury management in March 2012.[9] In April 2012, OFR finalized its longer-term Strategic Roadmap which lays out the expected evolution of OFR's capabilities through to the achievement of a mature state by fiscal year 2016. These documents, when supplemented with other planning documents and individual project plans produced by the Project Management Office, collectively provide OFR with a comprehensive implementation plan.

Concluding Remarks and Recommendation

As an observation, Dodd-Frank required Treasury to establish four new offices: OFR, the Consumer Financial Protection Bureau (CFPB),[10] a Federal Insurance Office, and an Office of Minority and Women Inclusion within DO.[11] We and the FRB OIG performed a joint review of CFPB's implementation planning activities. We reported on July 15, 2011, about a year after Dodd-Frank became law, that CFPB identified and documented implementation activities that were critical to standing up the agency's functions and necessary to address certain Dodd-Frank requirements.[12] CFPB did successfully stand up its operations on July 21, 2011, in accordance with Dodd-Frank; an accomplishment that we attribute to its comprehensive planning and implementation process. While we recognize OFR's mission is an entirely new undertaking for Treasury whereas CFPB, in part, consolidated existing government functions and personnel under one agency, the CFPB experience underscores the benefit of comprehensive planning for mission-critical and administrative activities necessary to stand up a new organization.

While progress has been made in laying the foundation for OFR's operational capabilities, OFR took longer than might have been expected to implement a project management capability and finalize a comprehensive implementation plan. OFR's operational success will depend, in part, on its ability to effectively execute its plan.

Accordingly, we recommend that the Chief Operating Officer of OFR monitor the progress in carrying out the activities in the comprehensive implementation plan and take timely action to address any slippages or otherwise make adjustments so as to achieve the objectives and timeframes in the plan.

Management Response

OFR will continue to monitor progress in carrying out the activities in its comprehensive implementation plan. OFR also plans to establish performance measures during fiscal year 2012, and implement them beginning in fiscal year 2013.

OIG Comment

OFR's planned action is responsive to our recommendation.

Jeffrey Dye /s/
Director, Banking Audits

APPENDIX 1. OBJECTIVE, SCOPE AND METHODOLOGY

The objective of this review is to determine the effectiveness of Treasury's process to establish the Office of Financial Research (OFR) in a manner which achieves the office's legislative mandates under the Dodd-Frank Wall Street Reform and Consumer Protection Act (Dodd-Frank).

To achieve the audit objective, we developed criteria using the applicable Dodd-Frank sections and best practices derived from various reports prepared by consultants and the Government Accountability Office[13]. Using these criteria, we reviewed documentation provided by OFR pertaining to the stand-up of OFR and interviewed key personnel. We:

- reviewed planning documentation provided by OFR related to: human resources, budget and finance, procurement, data collection and analysis, information security, technology infrastructure, and assessment functions. We also reviewed documentation pertaining to OFR's efforts to establish globally accepted legal entity identifiers (LEI).
- interviewed OFR management and Treasury Departmental Offices (DO) personnel detailed to or coordinating with OFR. Specifically, we interviewed the Counselor to the Secretary, who is the nominee for OFR Director, and the following OFR officials; Chief Operating Officer; Associate Director, Program Management; Chief Technology Officer, who was serving as Acting OFR Deputy Director – Data Center and Chief Business Officer; and Management Lead (DO reimbursable support). We also interviewed the DO Chief Information Security Officer, the Treasury Deputy General Counsel, and the DO Chief Human Capital Officer.

We performed our audit field work from June 2011 through April 2012.

We conducted this performance audit in accordance with generally accepted government auditing standards. Those standards require that we plan and perform the audit to obtain sufficient, appropriate evidence to provide a reasonable basis for our findings and conclusions based on our audit objectives. We believe that the evidence obtained provides a reasonable basis for our findings and conclusions based on our audit objectives.

End Notes

[1] FSOC, also established by Dodd-Frank, is charged with identifying threats to the financial stability of the U.S., promoting market discipline, and responding to emerging risks to the financial stability of the U.S. financial system. FSOC consists of 10 voting members and 5 nonvoting members. Its members include the Secretary of the Treasury, chief executives of the federal financial regulators, certain state financial regulators, and an insurance expert. The OFR Director is a nonvoting member of FSOC.

[2] LEI is being developed as the universal standard for identifying all parties to financial contracts. It is a key element in OFR's effort to understand and monitor risks to financial stability and meet its statutory mandate to develop and promote data standards.

[3] Section 155 (c), Interim Funding.

[4] Section 155 (d), Permanent Self Funding, defines large bank holding companies and nonbank financial companies as bank holding companies with total consolidated assets of $50 billion and nonbank financial companies supervised by FRB.

[5] Federal Register Volume 77, No. 98 (May 21, 2012), page 29884, Department of the Treasury, Assessment of Fees on Large Bank Holding Companies and Nonbank Financial Companies Supervised by the Federal Reserve Board To Cover the Expenses of the Financial Research Fund. The effective date for the final rule is July 20, 2012; the effective date for the interim final rule is July 20, 2012, with a due date for comments of September 18, 2012.

[6] Federal Register Volume 75, No. 229 (Nov. 30, 2010), page 74146, Office of Financial Research; Statement on Legal Entity Identification for Financial Contracts.

[7] GPRA, Pub. L. No. 103-62; and GPRA Modernization Act, Pub. L No. 111-352.

[8] Dodd-Frank, Sec. 154, Reporting Responsibilities, requires OFR to submit annual reports to Congress that assesses the state of the U.S. financial system, including (1) an analysis of any threats to the financial stability of the U.S., (2) the status of the efforts of OFR in meeting its mission, and (3) key findings from OFR's research and analysis of the financial system. The first report under this requirement is due July 21, 2012.

[9] OFR, *Strategic Framework Office of Financial Research FY 2012 - FY 2014*. OFR established five strategic goals consistent with its mandate defined in Dodd-Frank. These strategic goals are: (1) support the FSOC through the secure provision of high quality financial data and analysis needed to monitor threats to financial stability, (2) develop and promote data-related standards and best practices, (3) establish a center for excellence for research on financial stability and promote best practices for financial risk management, (4) provide the public with key data and analysis, while protecting sensitive information, and (5) establish the OFR as an efficient organization and a world-class workplace.

[10] Dodd-Frank established CFPB as an independent agency within, but autonomous from, the Federal Reserve System. Treasury was authorized to provide interim administrative services supporting CFPB before July 21, 2011.

[11] Dodd-Frank also required the Office of the Comptroller of the Currency to establish an Office of Minority and Women Inclusion. We plan to review the Federal Insurance Office and the Offices of Minority and Women Inclusion in the future.

[12] Treasury OIG and FRB OIG, *Review of CFPB Implementation Planning Activities*, FRB OIG 2011-03/OIG-11-088 (July 15, 2011)

[13] Booz Allen Hamilton – Research and Analysis: Organizational Stand-Ups Lessons Learned and Key Insights (May 2010); and General Accountability Office – GAO-03-669, Results Oriented Cultures: Implementation Steps to Assist Mergers and Organizational Transformations (July 2003)

INDEX

A

B

C

D

E

F

G

H

I

L

R

S

T

U

V

W